TIDAL [illegible]HES

Written & Illustrated by

Margaret Merry

Published by Margaret Merry
19 Carne Meadows, Tresillian
Truro, Cornwall. TR2 4BQ

ISBN 0 948752 03 3

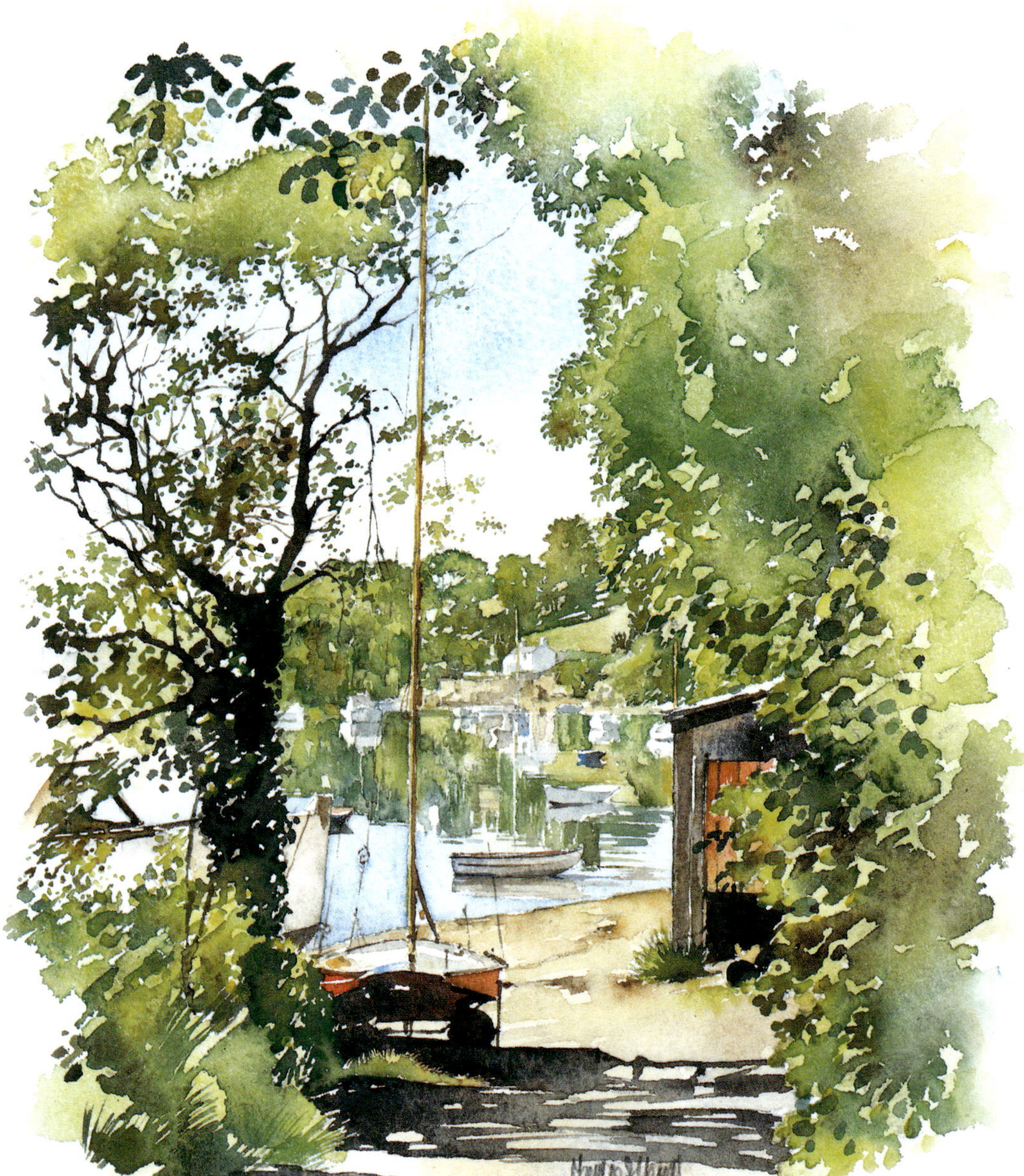

Pill Creek, near Feock

For many people, Cornwall's attraction is the glorious scenery of the Atlantic coast: wide, sandy beaches swept by great breakers and towering cliffs pounded by heaving seas. For me, though, it is the gentler aspect of the sheltered south coast which appeals. The little coves, fishing villages and harbours and the river estuaries with their secluded creeks and thickly wooded banks are my favourite haunts.

It was childhood Summer holidays spent with my cousin in Brixham which began my fascination with fishing ports. I loved the atmosphere, the bustle, the all-pervading fishy smells, the ceaseless wailing of the gulls and the intense colours, accentuated by the reflected light of the sun on the water, of the brightly painted boats. Later on, when I was growing up in Falmouth, I grew to love the tranquil beauty of the natural scenery of the Fal and Helford estuaries with their diversity of wildlife and the ever changing effects of the tides and the weather.

It is these subjects which have provided me with inspiration for most of my work throughout my career as an artist.

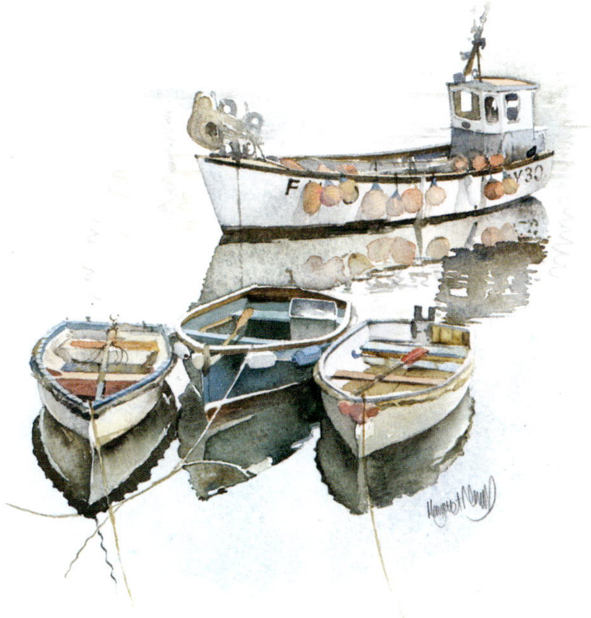

Fishing boats at Mevagissey

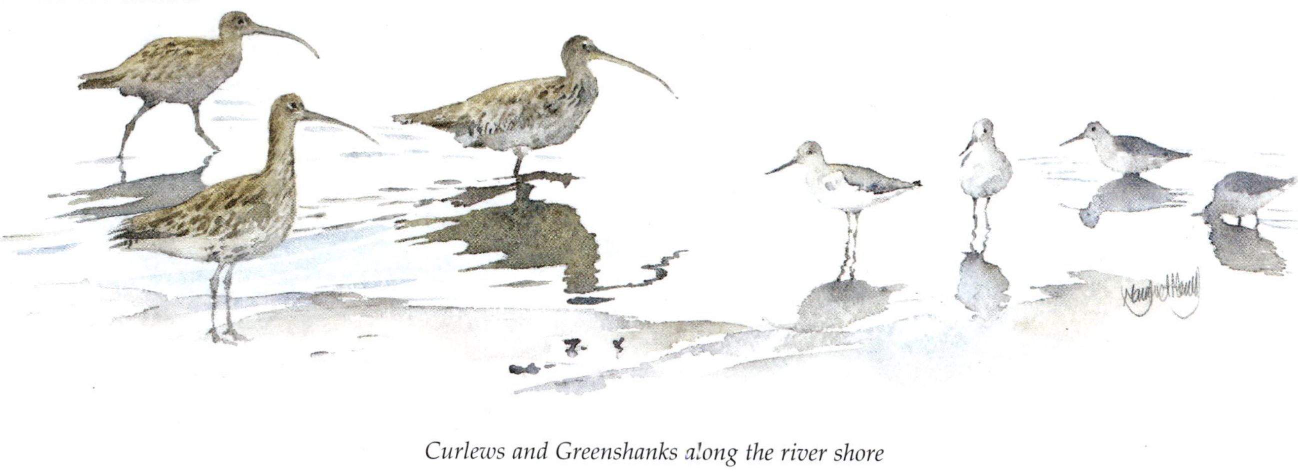

Curlews and Greenshanks along the river shore

MOUNTS BAY & WEST PENWITH

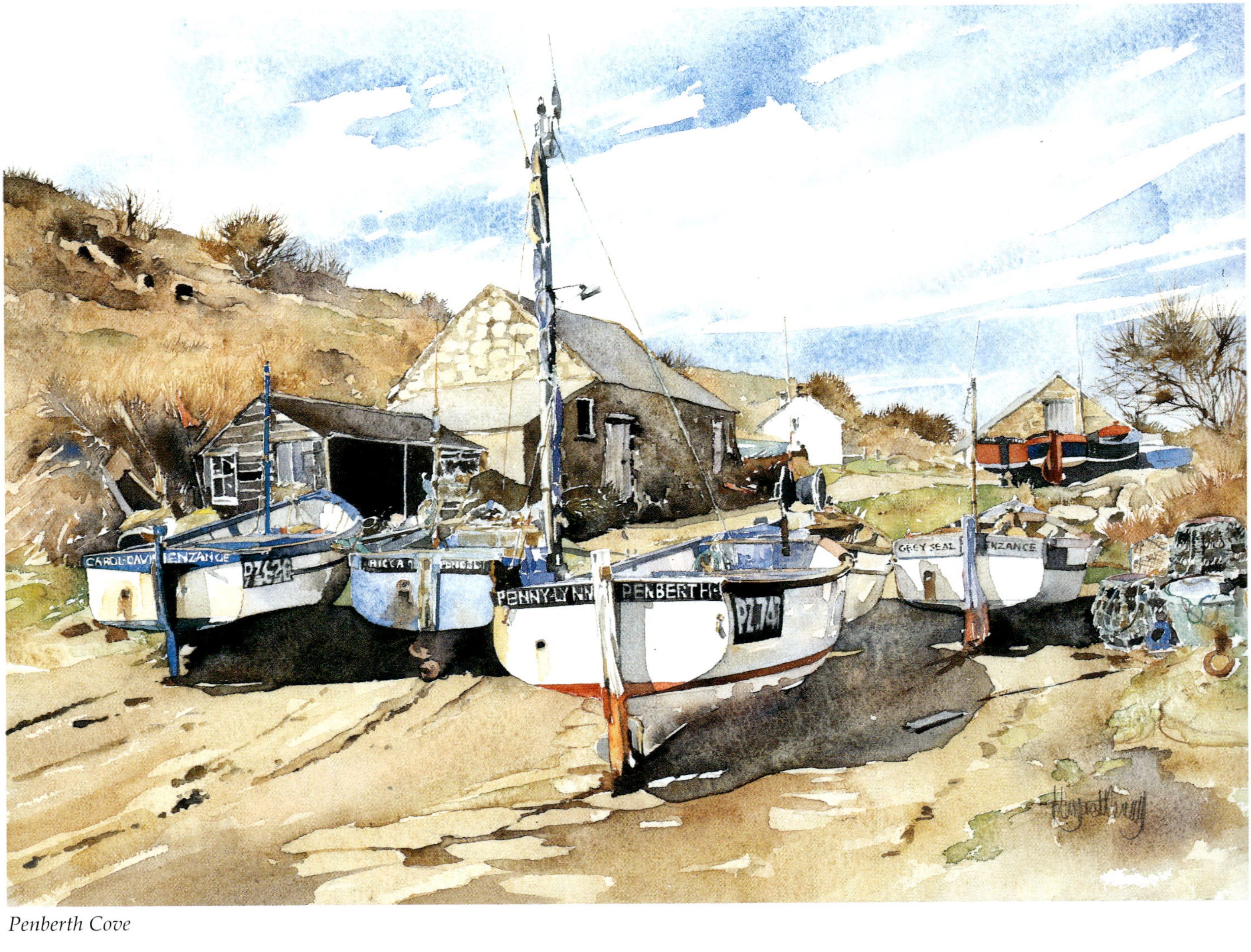

Penberth Cove

West of Penzance is Treen; a cluster of pretty cottages, it is not so much a hamlet as a flower garden. Walking through this lush valley, you eventually come to Penberth Cove and here, among the groups of colourful fishing boats in their setting of granite boulders, far removed from the clamour of modern life, you have the distinct feeling that you have stepped back in time and have found yourself in one of those small Cornish fishing communities typical of bygone days.

On fine days, when you look out to sea at the water shimmering in the sunlight, you are able to appreciate the legendary quality of light which has lured so many artists to West Cornwall.

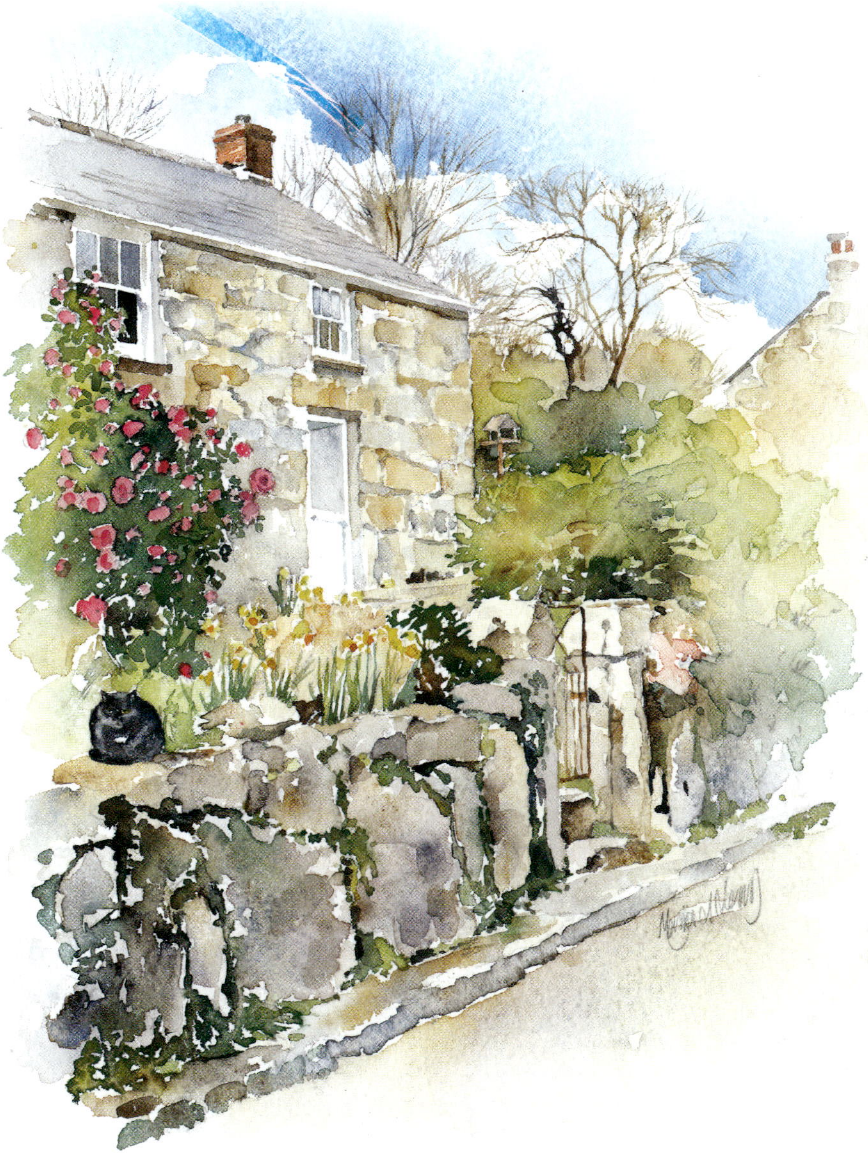

Cottages at Treen

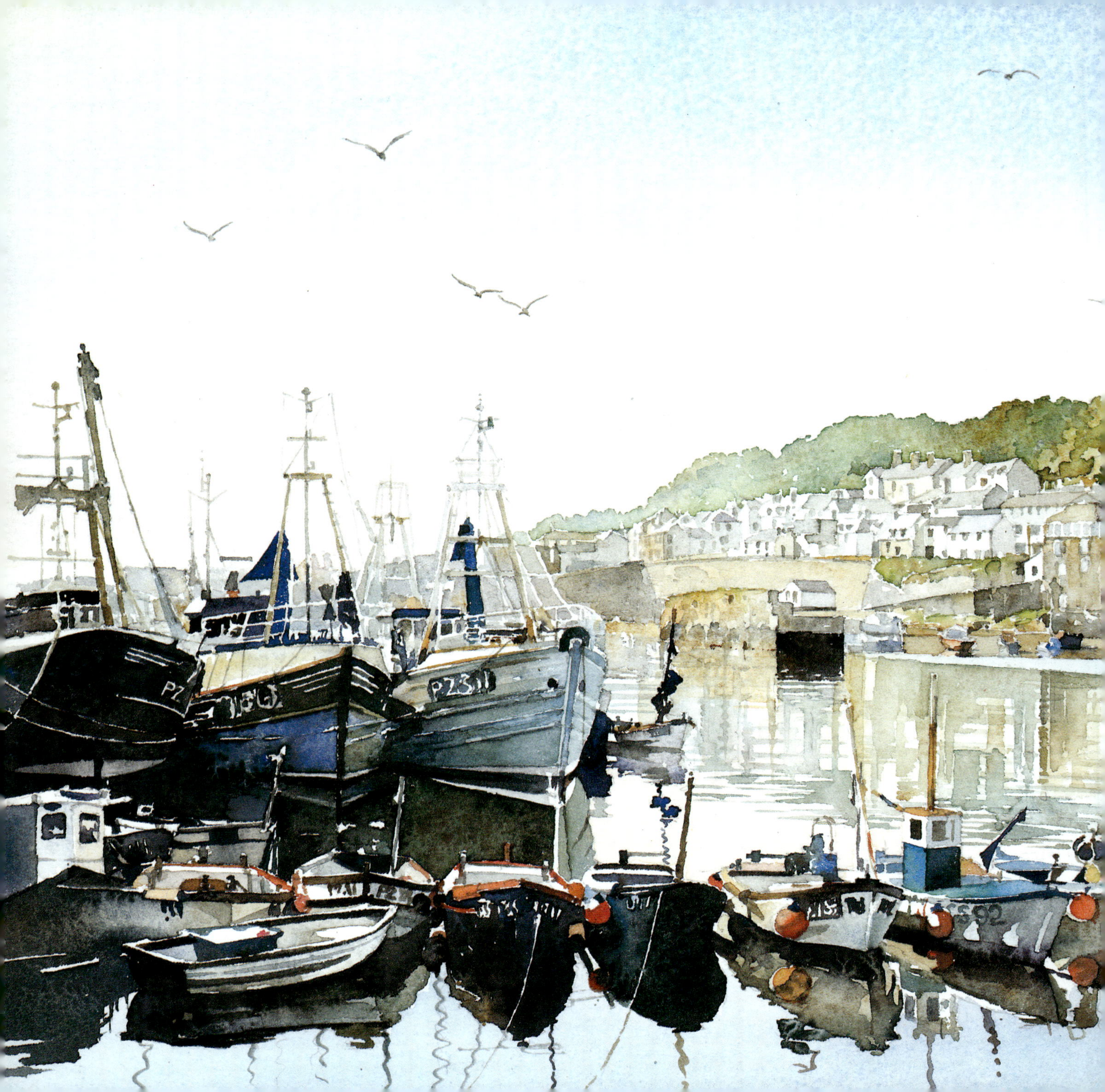

Despite modern development and the effects of tourism, there still remains something of the charm of the old Newlyn which attracted the painters of the famous Newlyn School in Edwardian times. Today's artists can still find inspiration in the narrow streets, the granite cottages with their medley of chimney pots, the weathered harbour walls and huddles of old buildings, the bustling and colourful fishing fleet (though now much diminished) and, of course, the imposing view of St. Michael's Mount in the bay beyond.

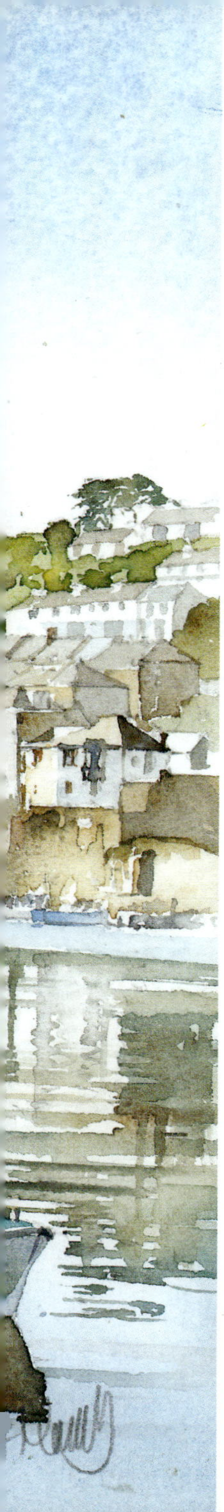

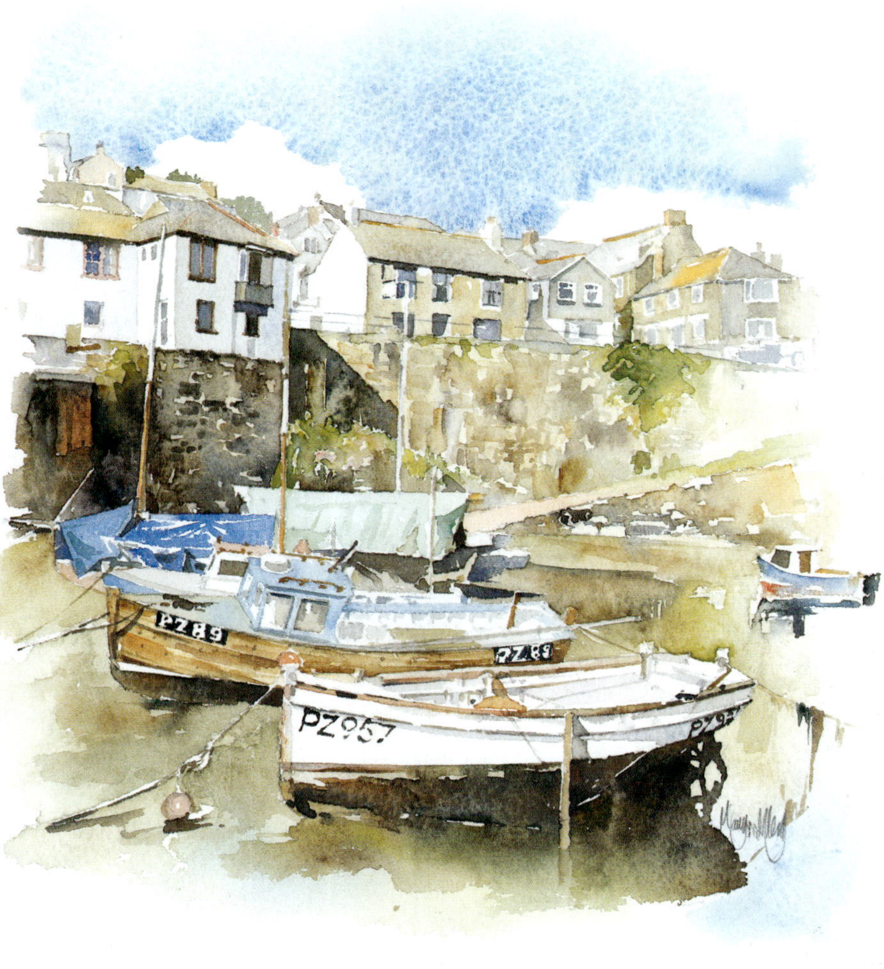

Views of Newlyn harbour

Unlike Truro, which has lost most of its character to development, Penzance still retains the quiet dignity of a Georgian town with its elegant regency terraces and long promenade and its abundance of sub-tropical plants are proof of its mild winter climate.

St. Mary's parish church rises above the town and dominates this view of the harbour, busy with commercial and pleasure craft on a bright summer's day.

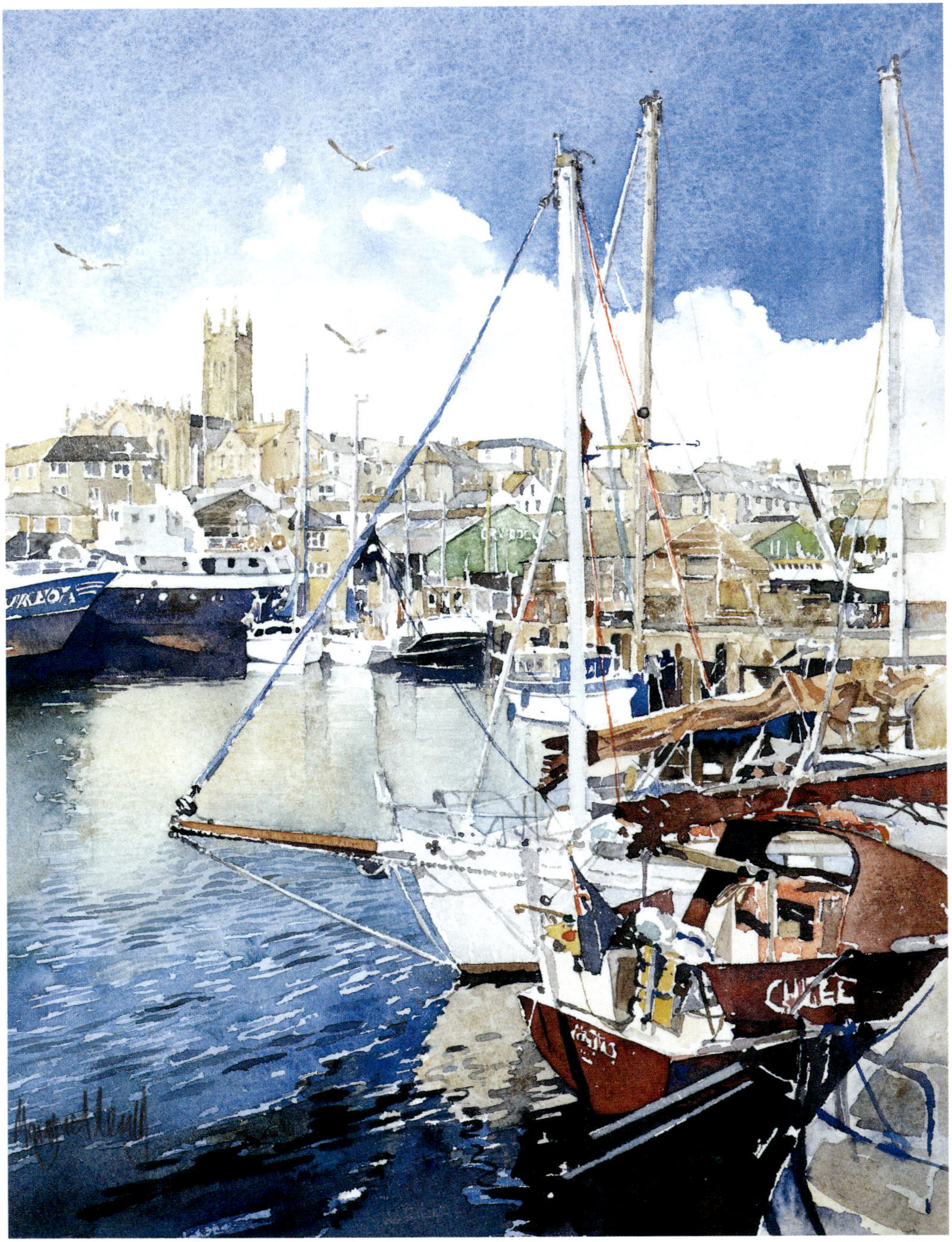

Penzance harbour

No other image is quite so evocative of Cornwall as that of St. Michael's Mount and it has been painted countless times. However, I don't think it is a particularly easy subject as, if seen from a distance, it can look rather like a molehill; to avoid this effect I would use a low horizon and a dramatic sky to give it significance. Here, the mount dominates the picture and shows the causeway which allows pedestrian access at low tide.

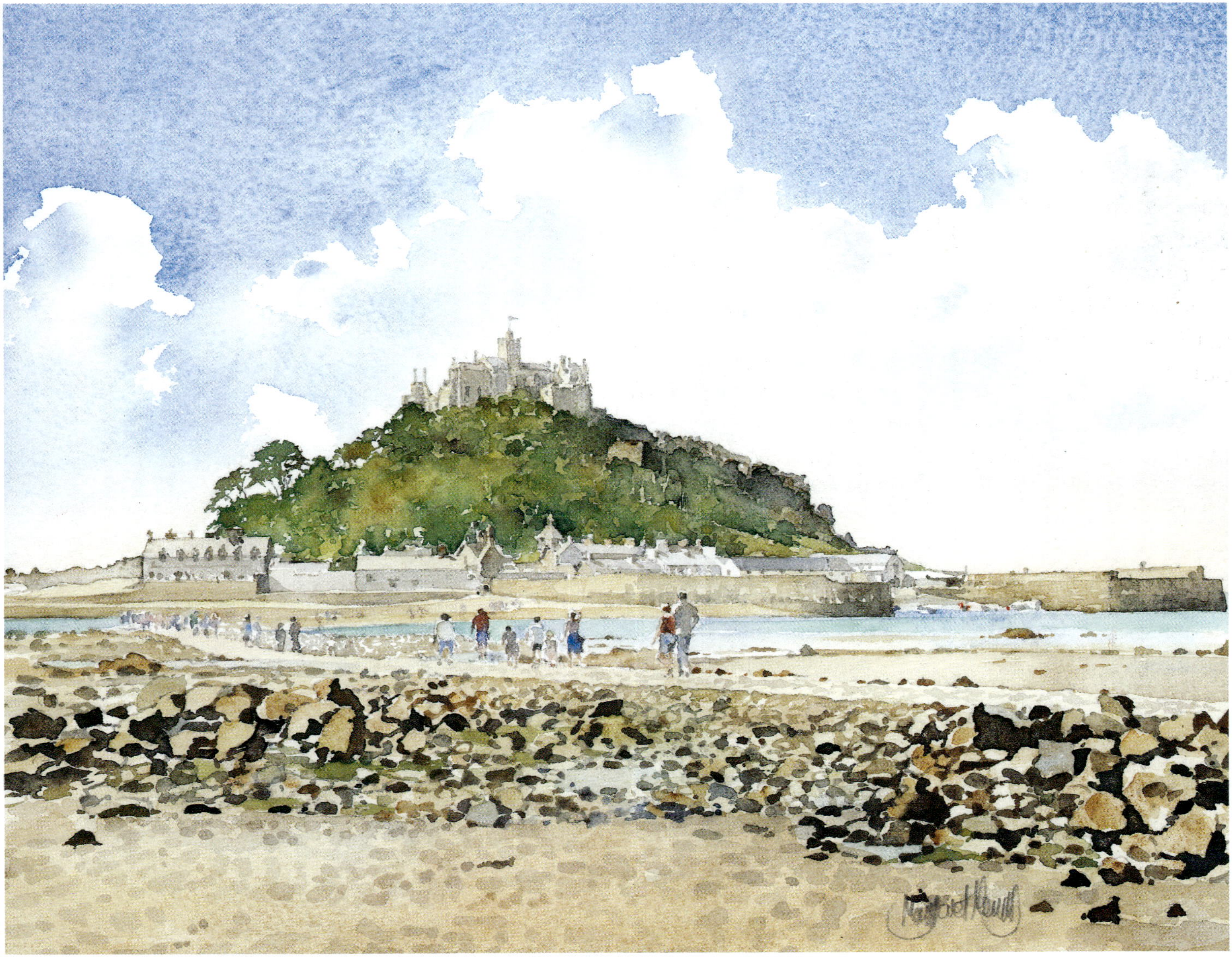

St. Michael's Mount

THE LIZARD

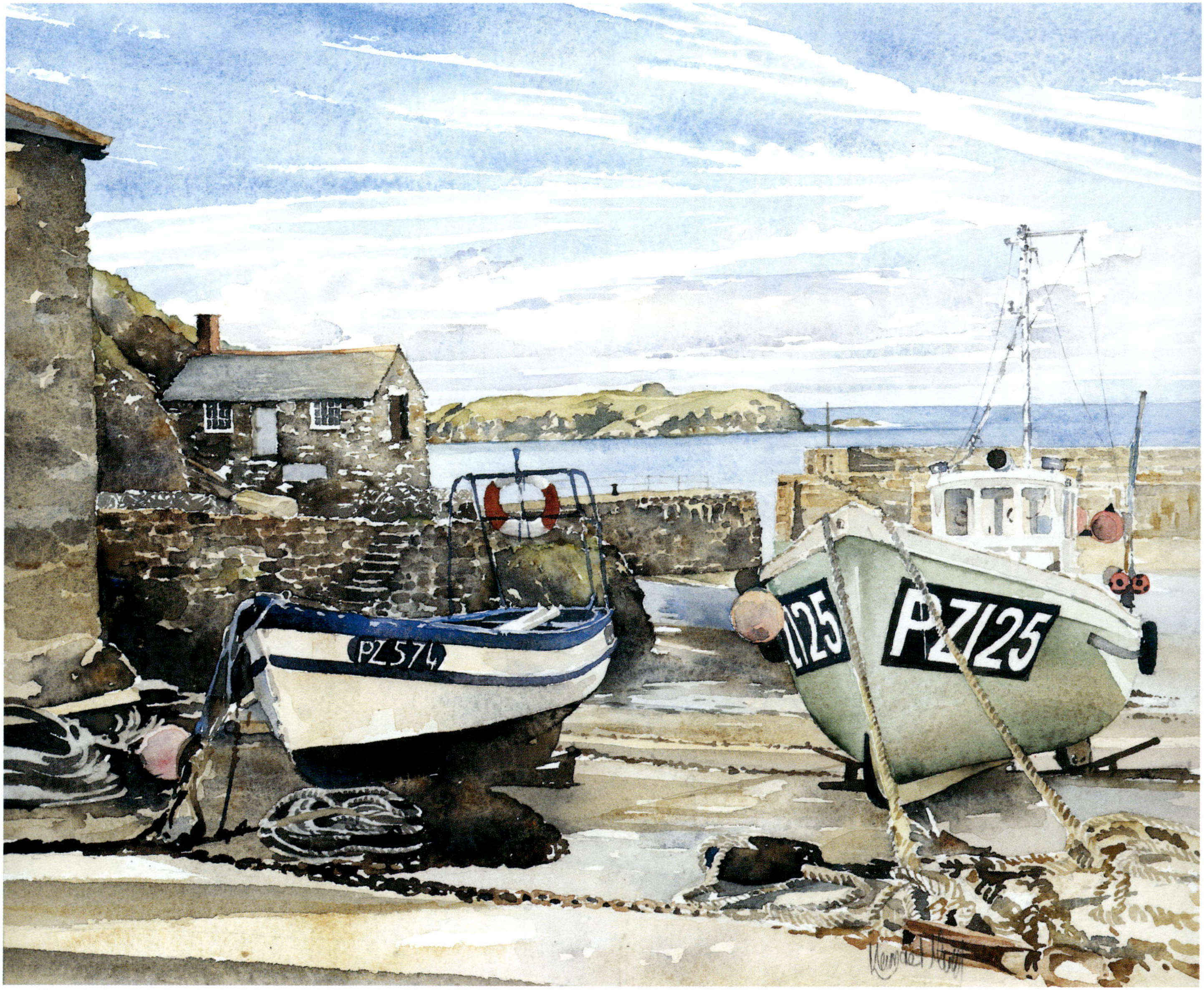

Mullion Cove

Cornwall's southernmost peninsula, the Lizard, is set apart from the rest of the county by the complicated nature of its geology and I think this is the reason for the feeling of remoteness that the region generates; it is this atmosphere and sense of being different which attracts as much as the splendour of the scenery and I have been drawn to this place ever since I was a child. Mullion cove was one of the first harbour scenes I ever painted and it seems to have changed little over the years. It makes such a perfect composition with the boats in the foreground, the old, weathered building on the left, Mullion Island and the spectacular coastal scenery beyond the stone jetties that little artistic licence is required.

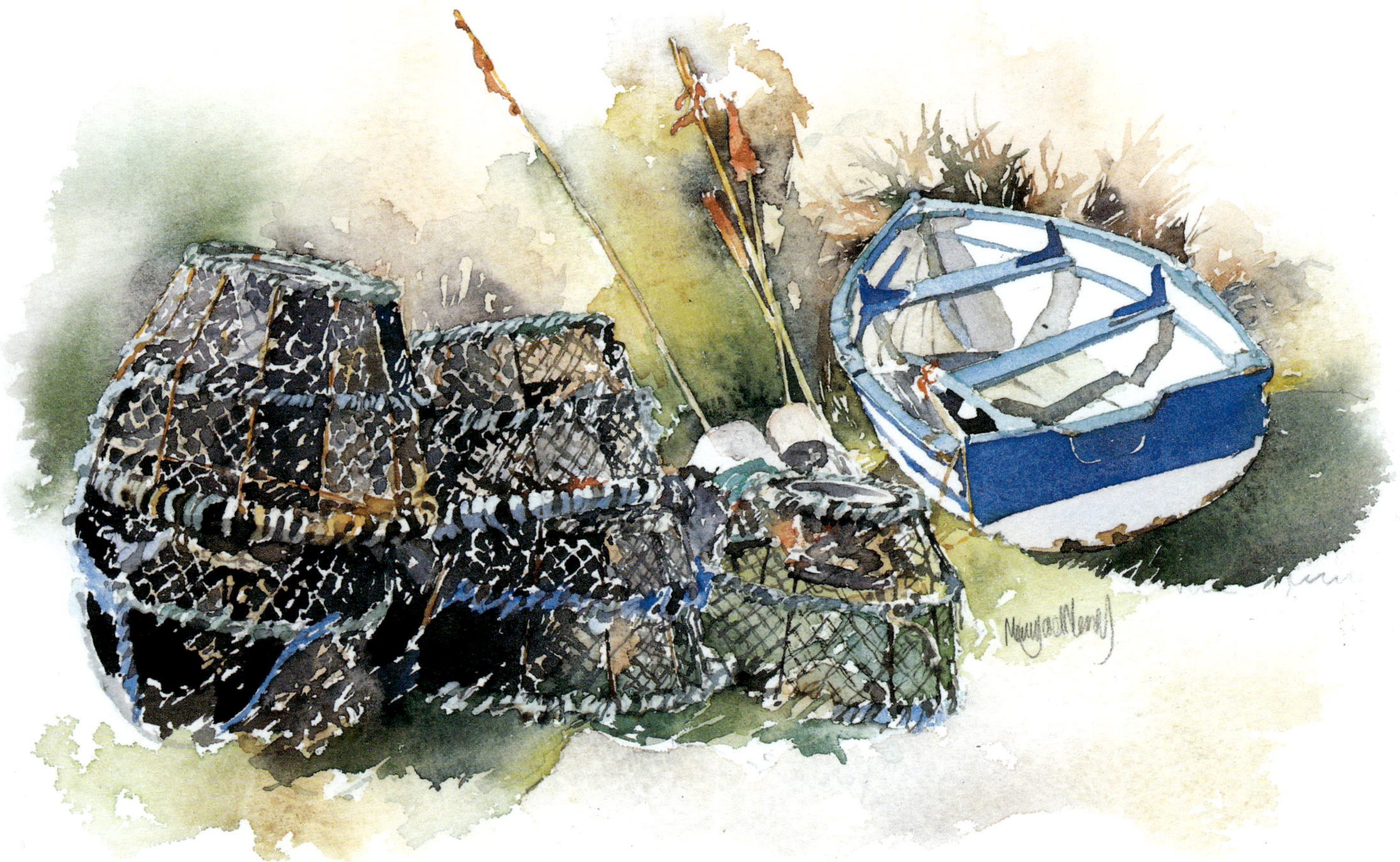

It is unusual to see so many thatched cottages in Cornwall as there are in Cadgwith and this is probably the reason why it is such a picturesque place. Tourism has taken the place of the once thriving fishing economy but there are still boats winched up above the high tide mark on the beach. The Lizard is one of the most important areas in Britain for wild flowers and the cliff paths around Cadgwith especially are a botanist's delight.

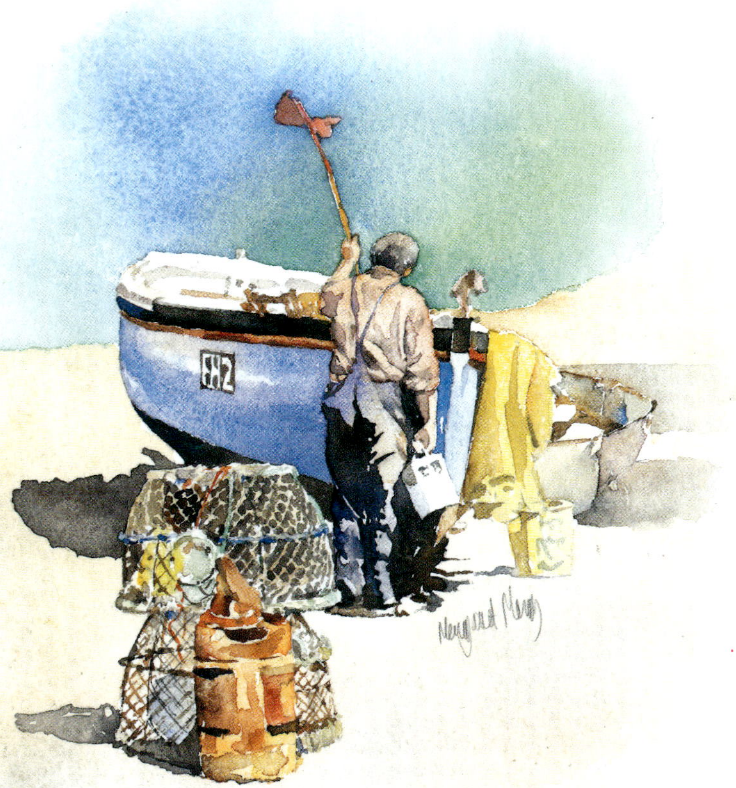

Cadgwith

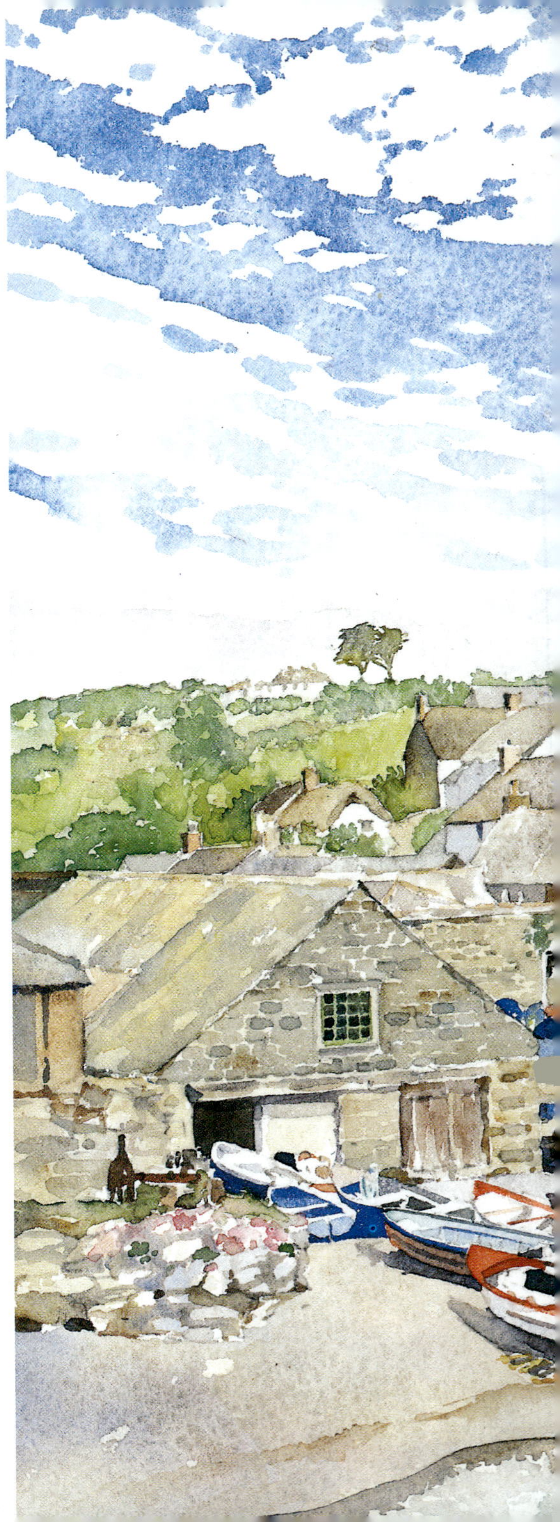

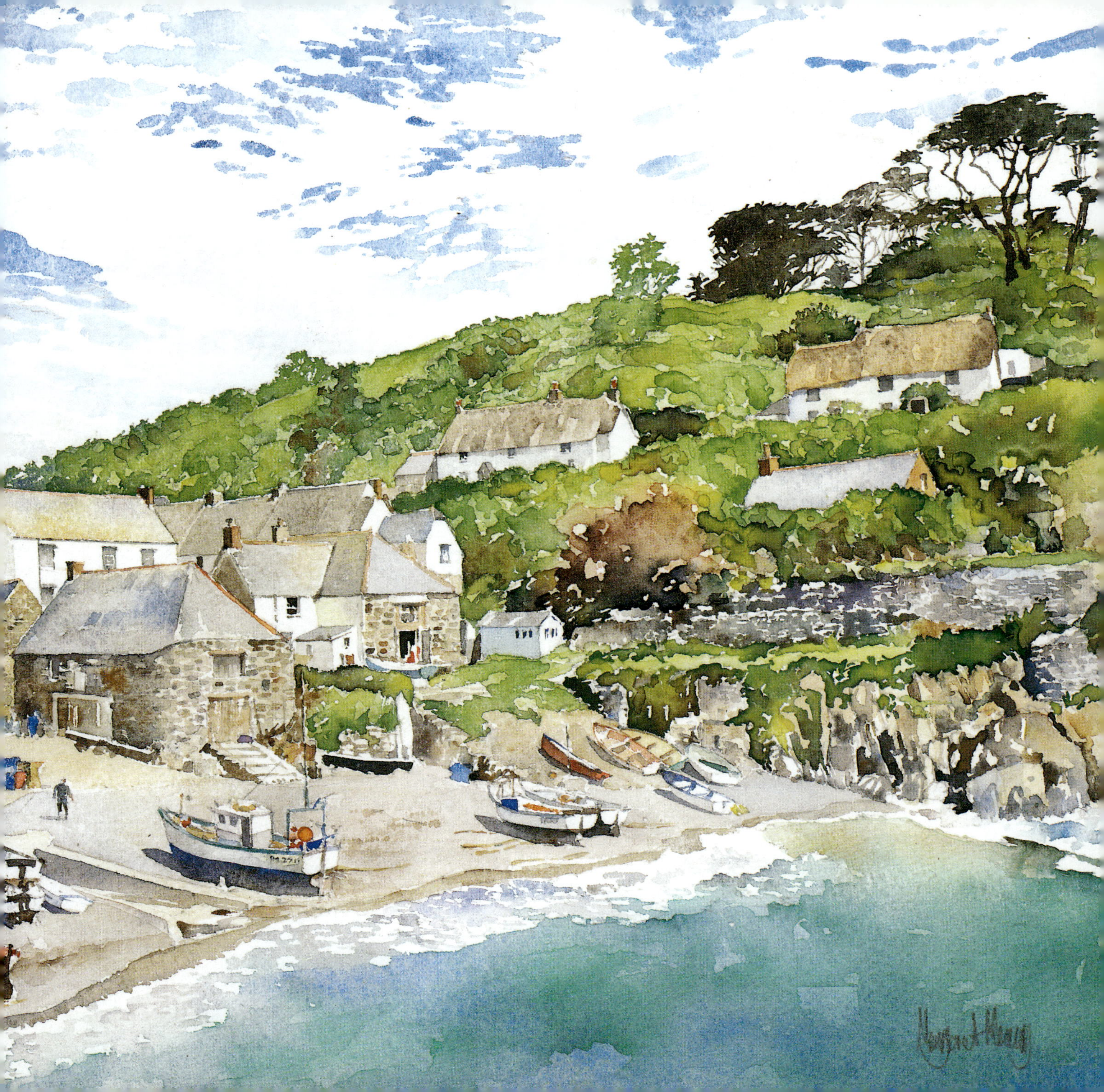

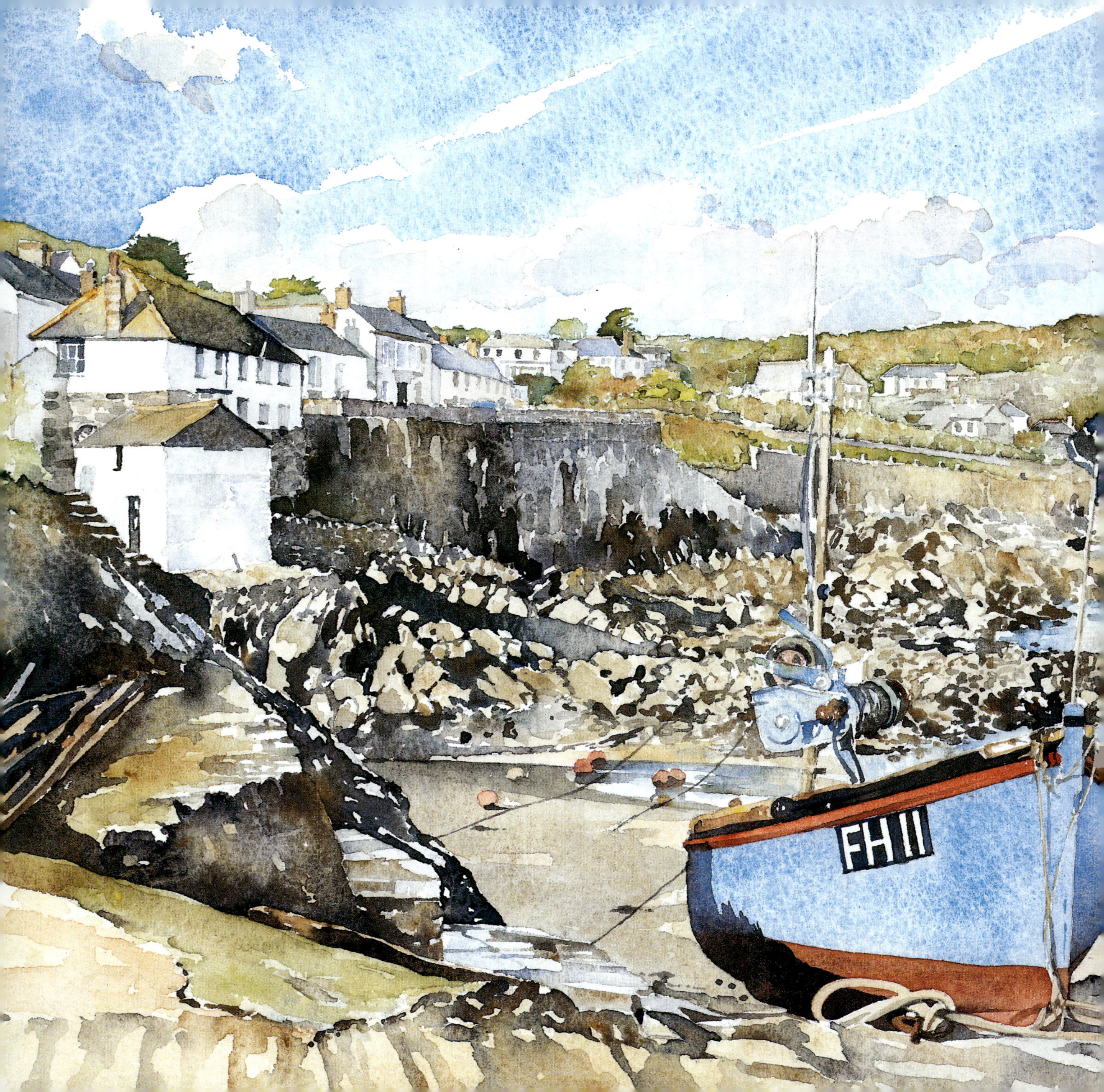
FH 11

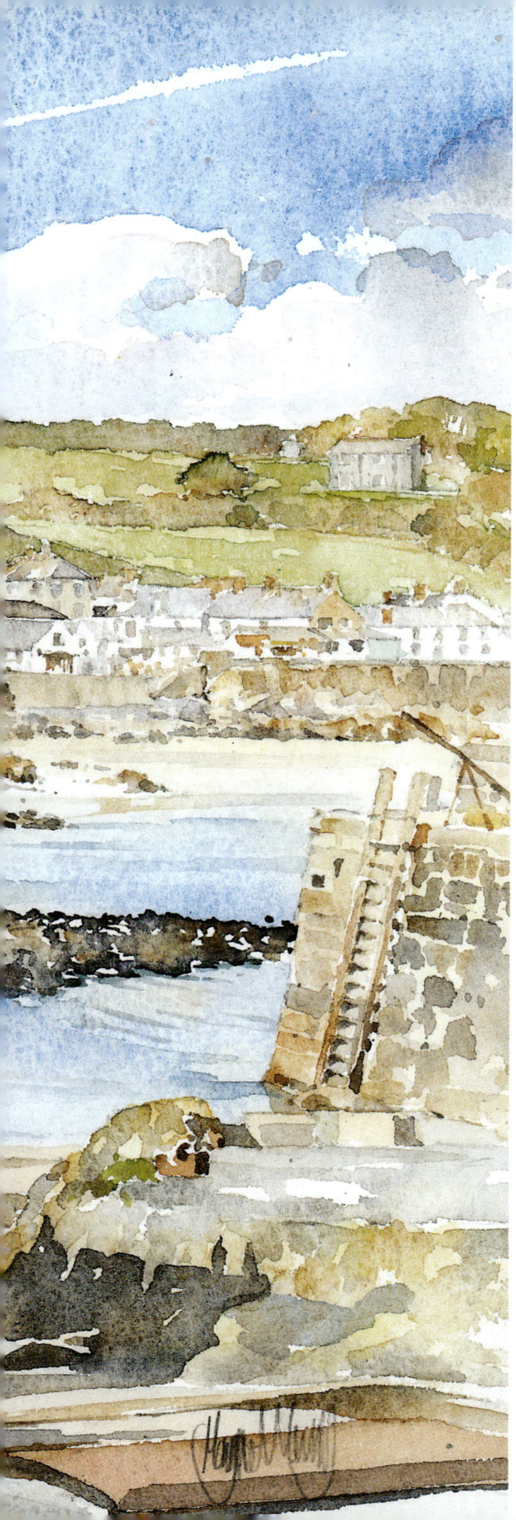

Although very much a tourist resort, Coverack still retains its Cornish character and a feeling of its smuggling past. I have always liked this view of the jetty and cluster of old buildings on the left with the beach and the sea in the distance.

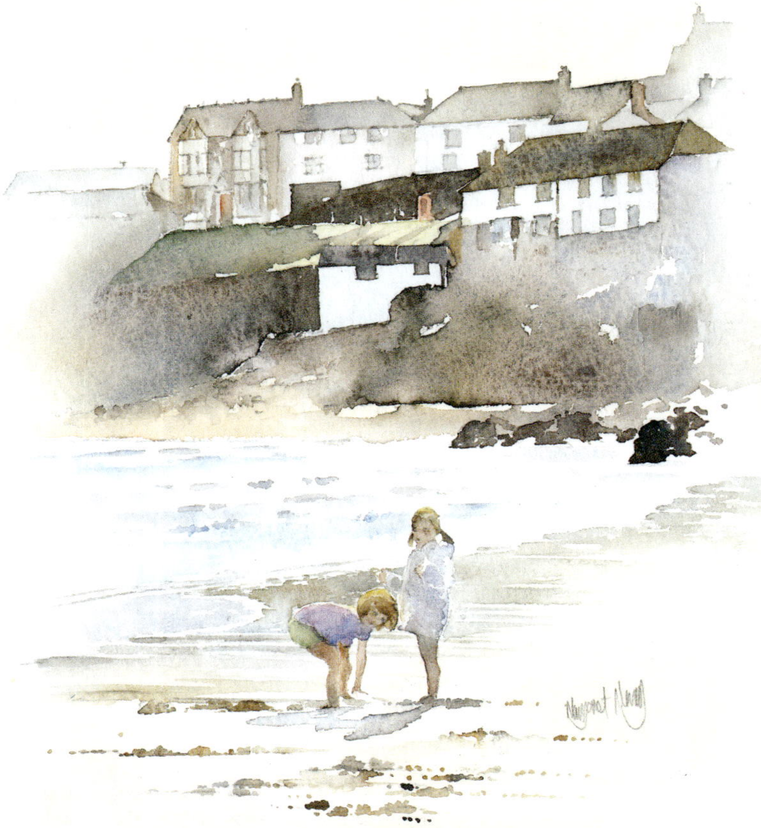

Coverack

THE HELFORD RIVER

The luxuriant greenery of the sheltered Helford river is very different from the remote and rugged beauty of the rest of the Lizard. From mid-May, when Cornwall is at its most beautiful, until late autumn before the trees have lost their leaves, you cannot travel very far without finding inspiration in its pretty riverside villages, secluded creeks or famous valley gardens lush with exotic plants.

Narrow, high-banked lanes descend to the creekside church at St. Anthony. So many boats line the foreshore that you have to walk along the road and onto a little beach in order to get a good view, as I have done here. The painting was done in late April when the surrounding oaks were just coming into leaf.

St. Anthony in Meneage

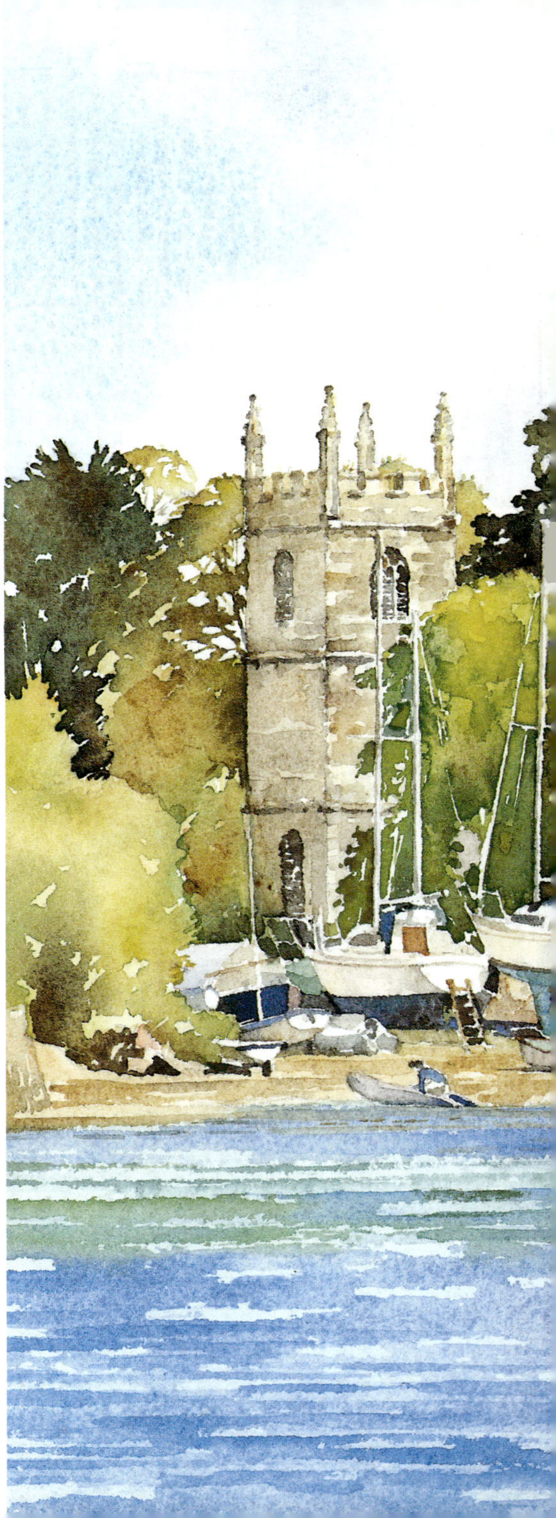

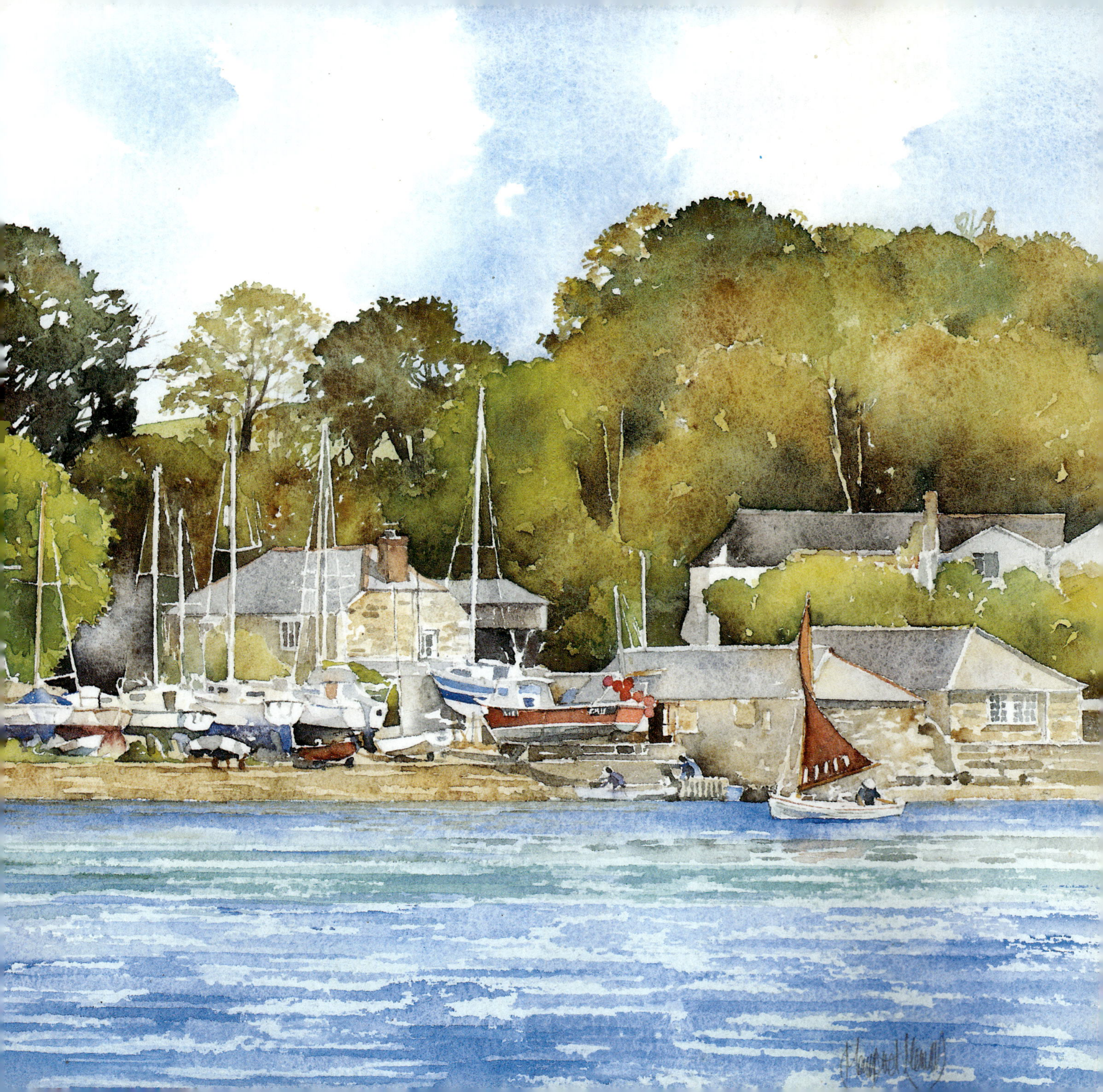

When I was a child, I would often accompany my father on trips around the Helford to buy produce from nurseries and smallholdings for his greengrocery shop in Falmouth. I loved the flowery, high-banked lanes with their glimpses of creeks and river views and Gweek was one of my favourite places. It is the furthermost tidal reach of the Helford river and although the creek is silted up, there are lots of boats to make interesting compositions for paintings.

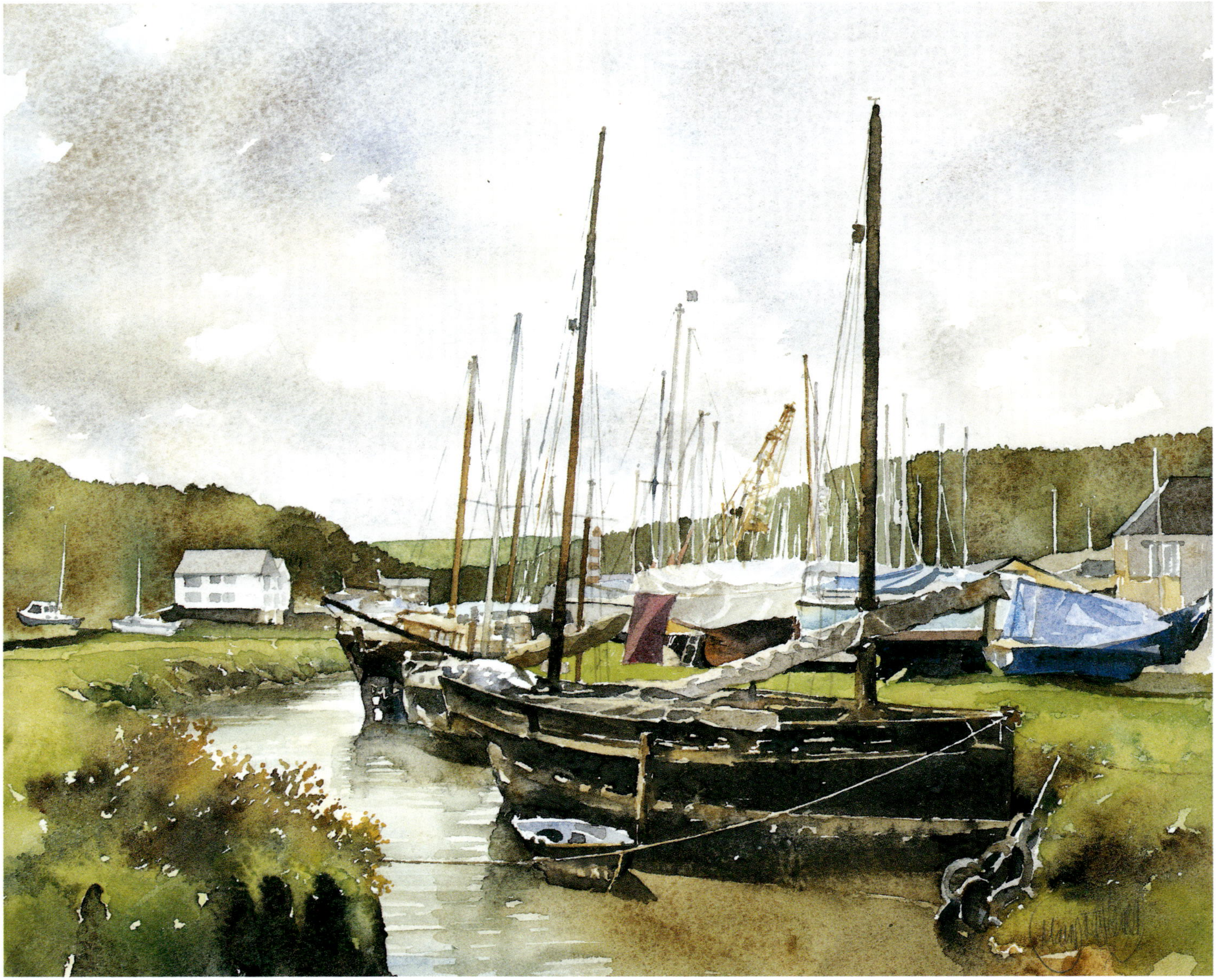

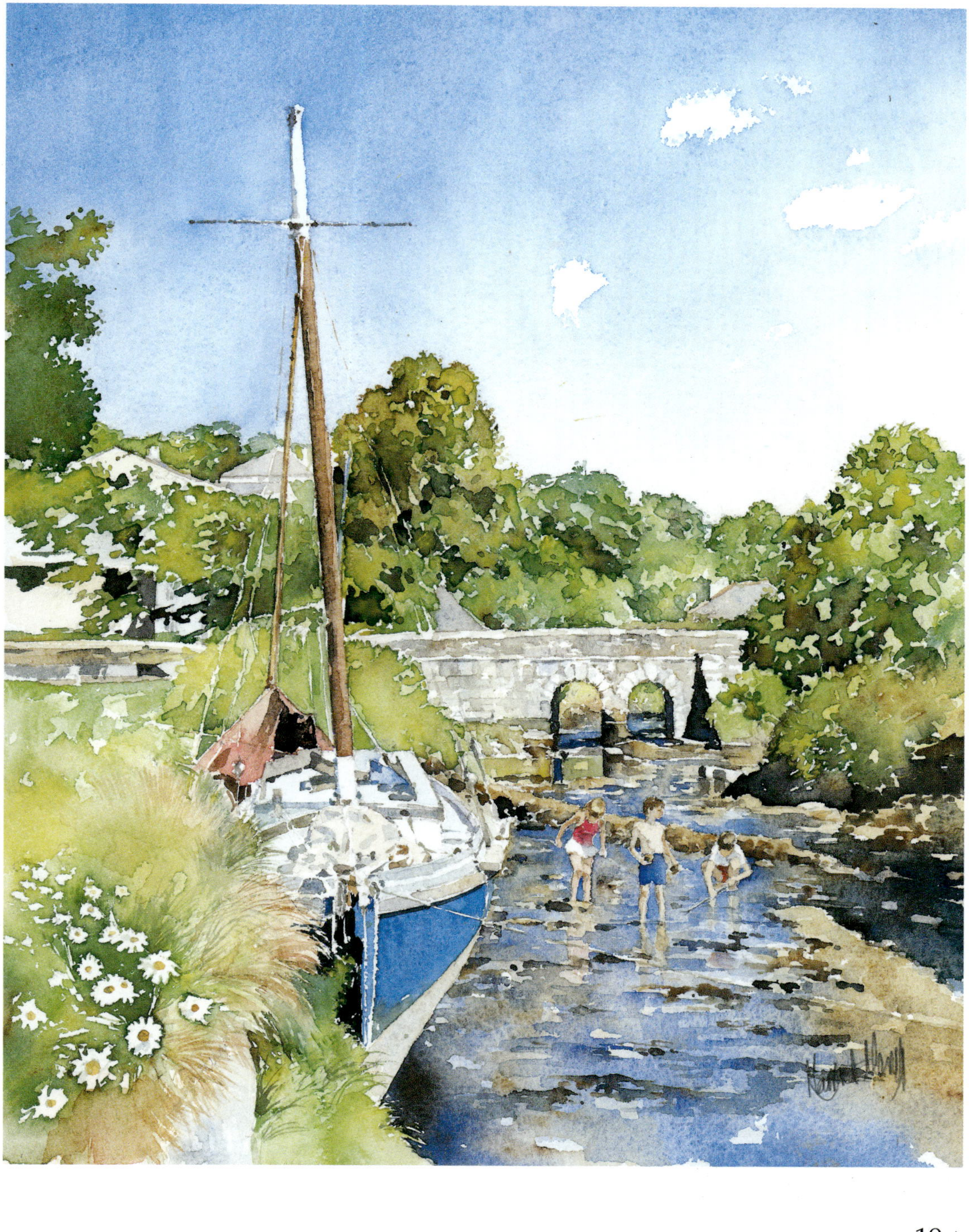

Two views of Gweek

The popular Ferryboat Inn was once a passage house where travellers could stop to take a drink while they waited for the ferry to take them across the water to Helford. Walking across the fields on a summer's evening, you can hear in the distance the voices of the crowds that spill out across the road and onto the beach where brightly coloured boats are moored. On top of the hill, the row of cottages with the pines behind them and the beach with all its activity in the foreground contrive to make this scene an attractive composition.

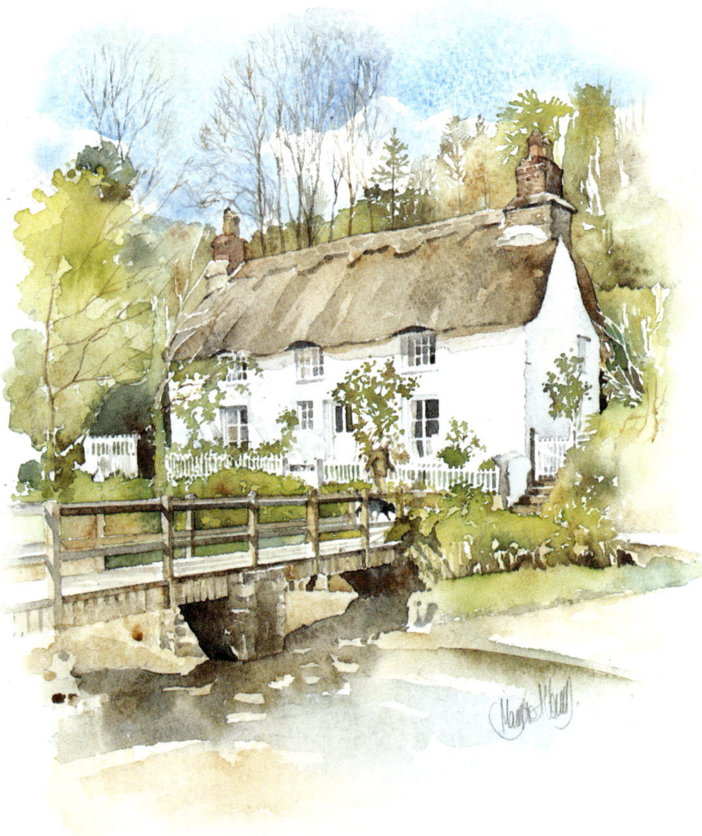

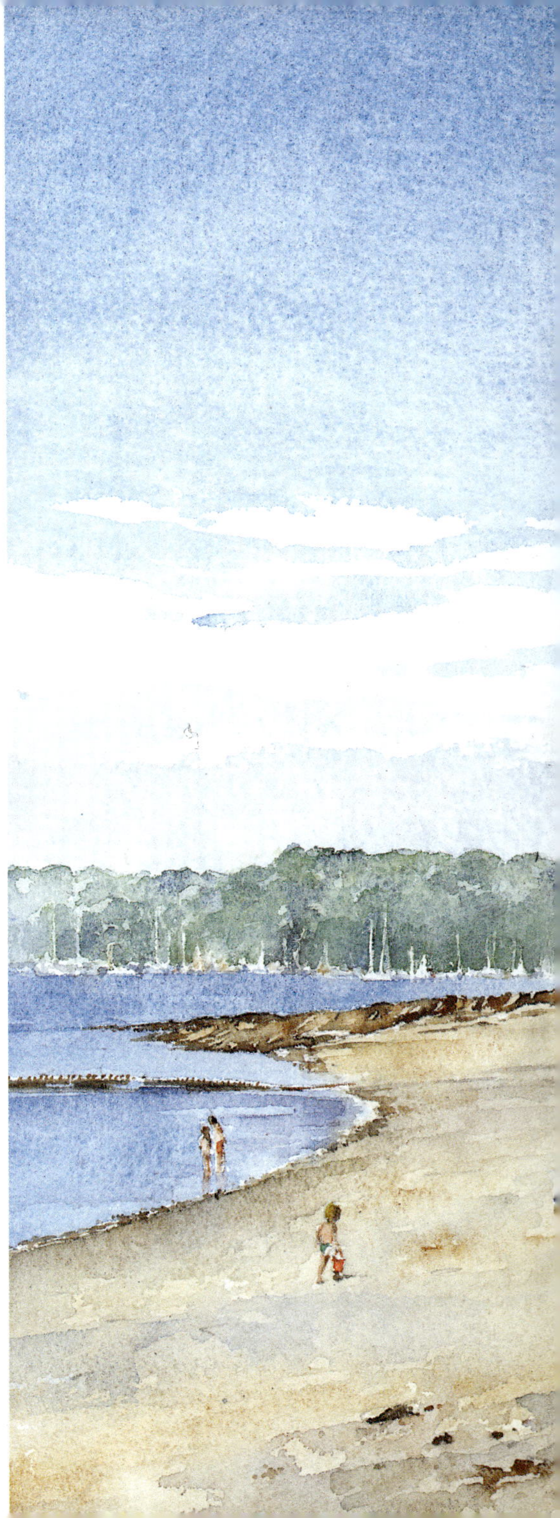

Cottage at Helford village and Helford Passage and the Ferryboat Inn

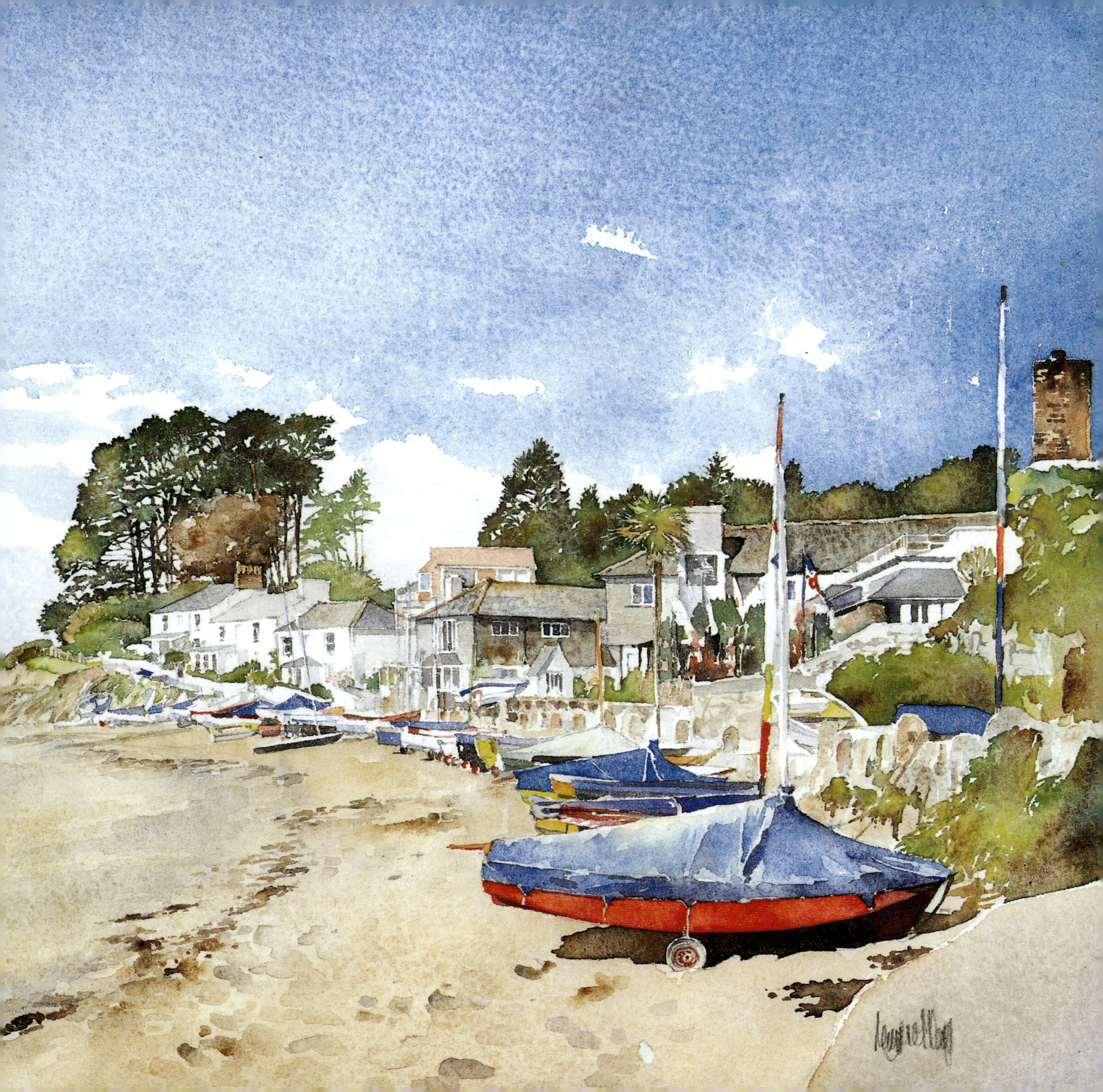

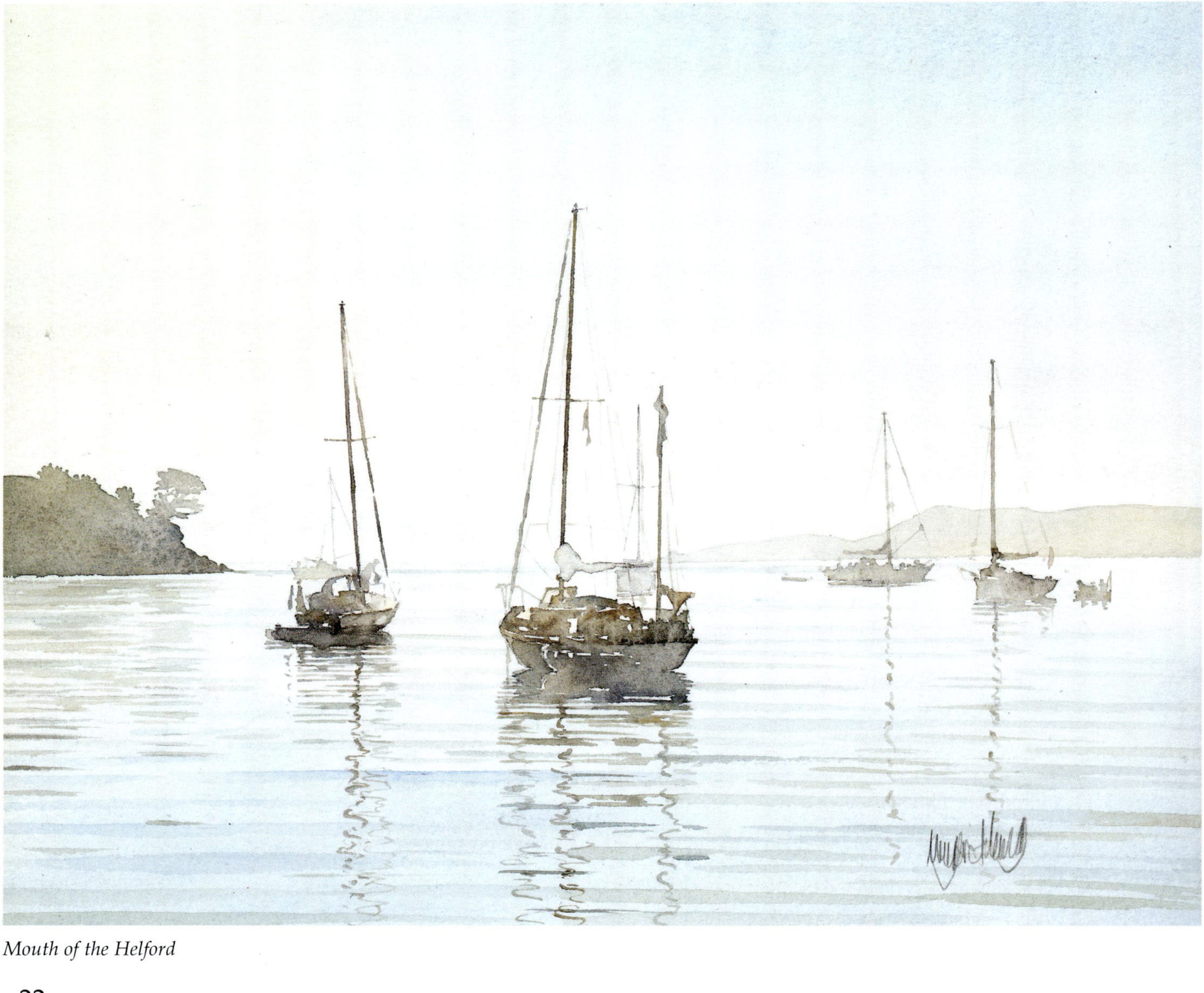

Mouth of the Helford

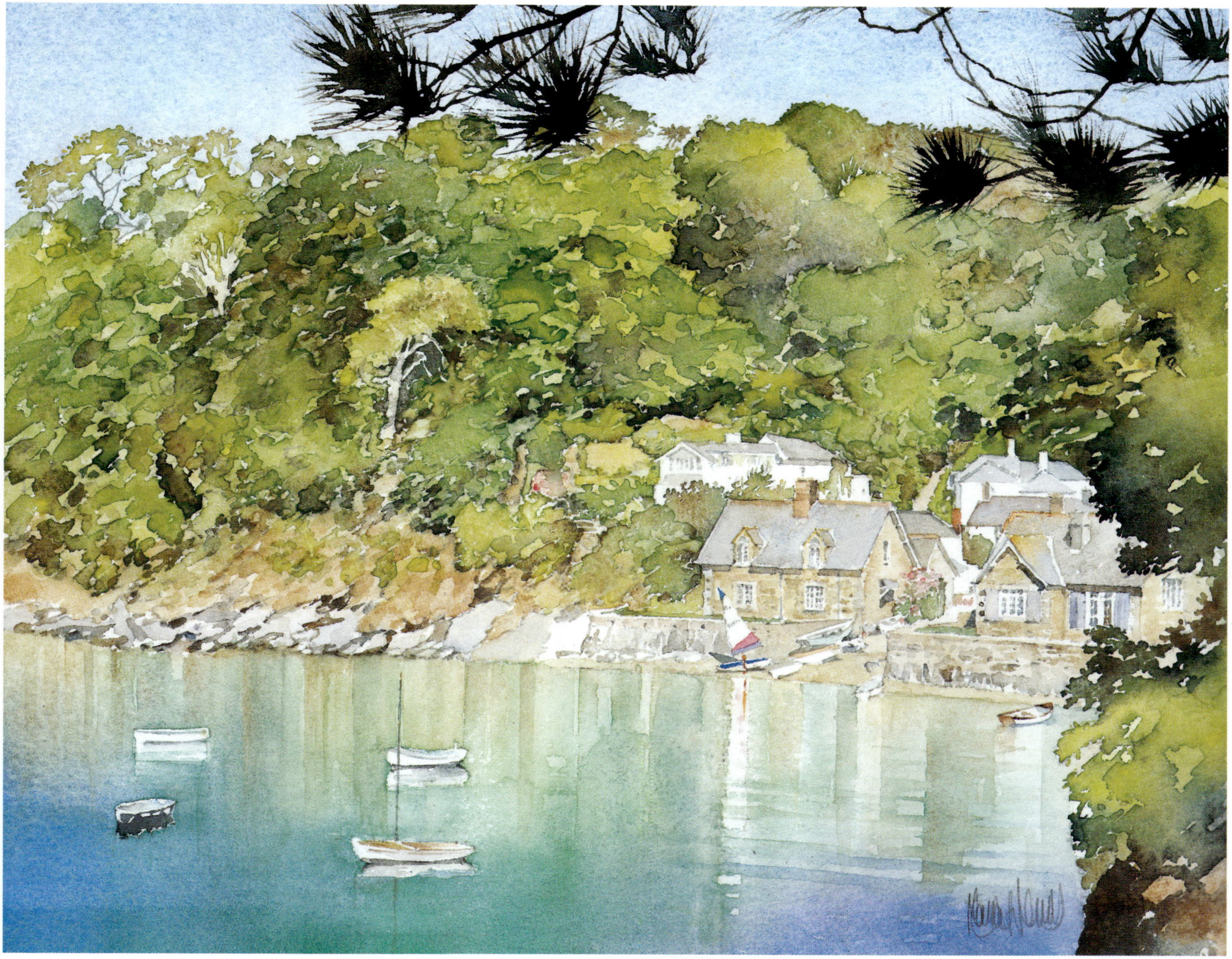

Durgan

One August day I overheard a resident of Durgan say that he couldn't understand why, since the place was so small and quiet, it attracted so many people. I think the reason is its sentimental value; people who spent happy times here as children return as adults year after year to rediscover pleasant associations. This view, from the top of the steep hill that descends into the village, with the transparent, turquoise water in the foreground, is the best one to paint.

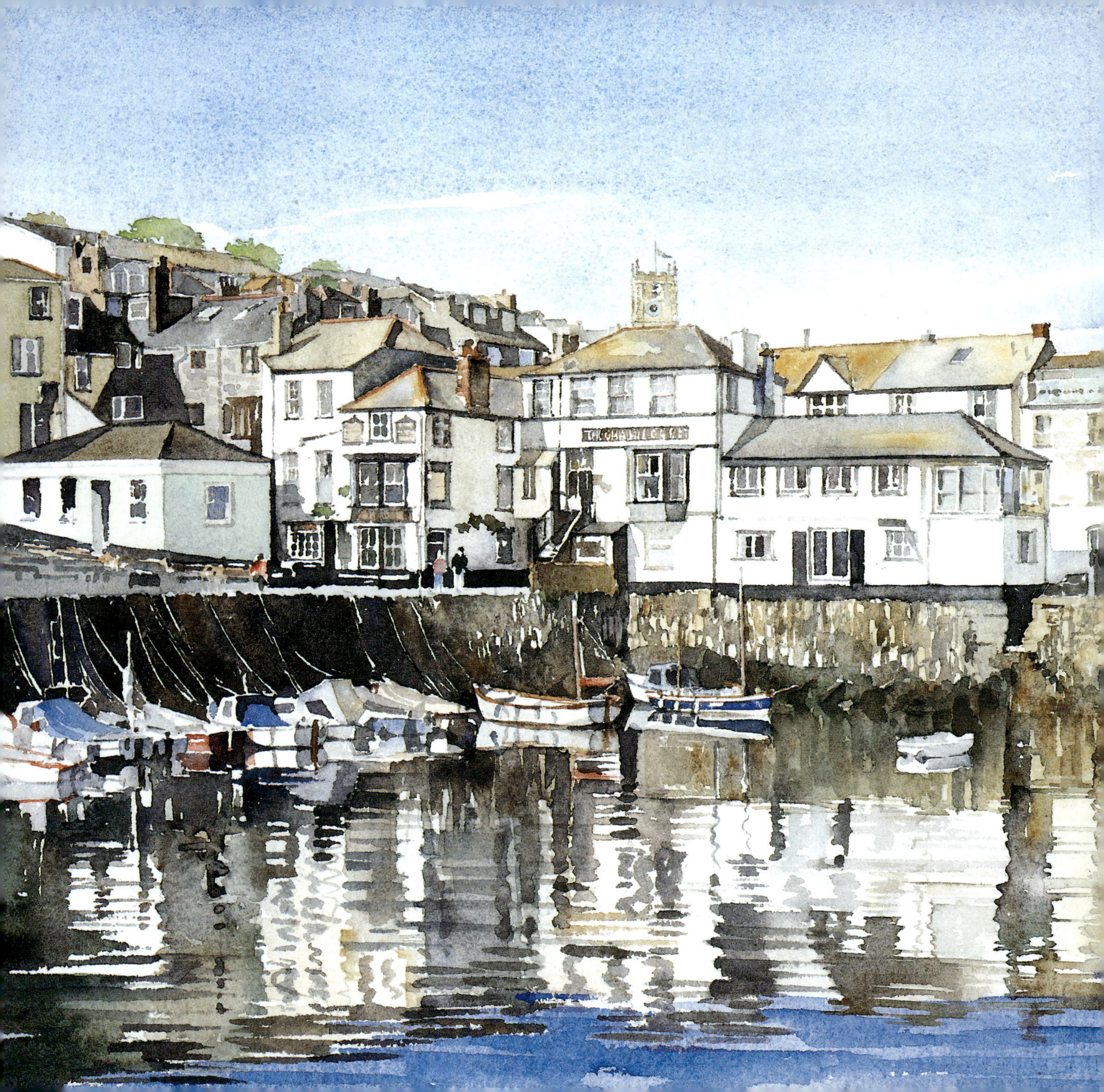

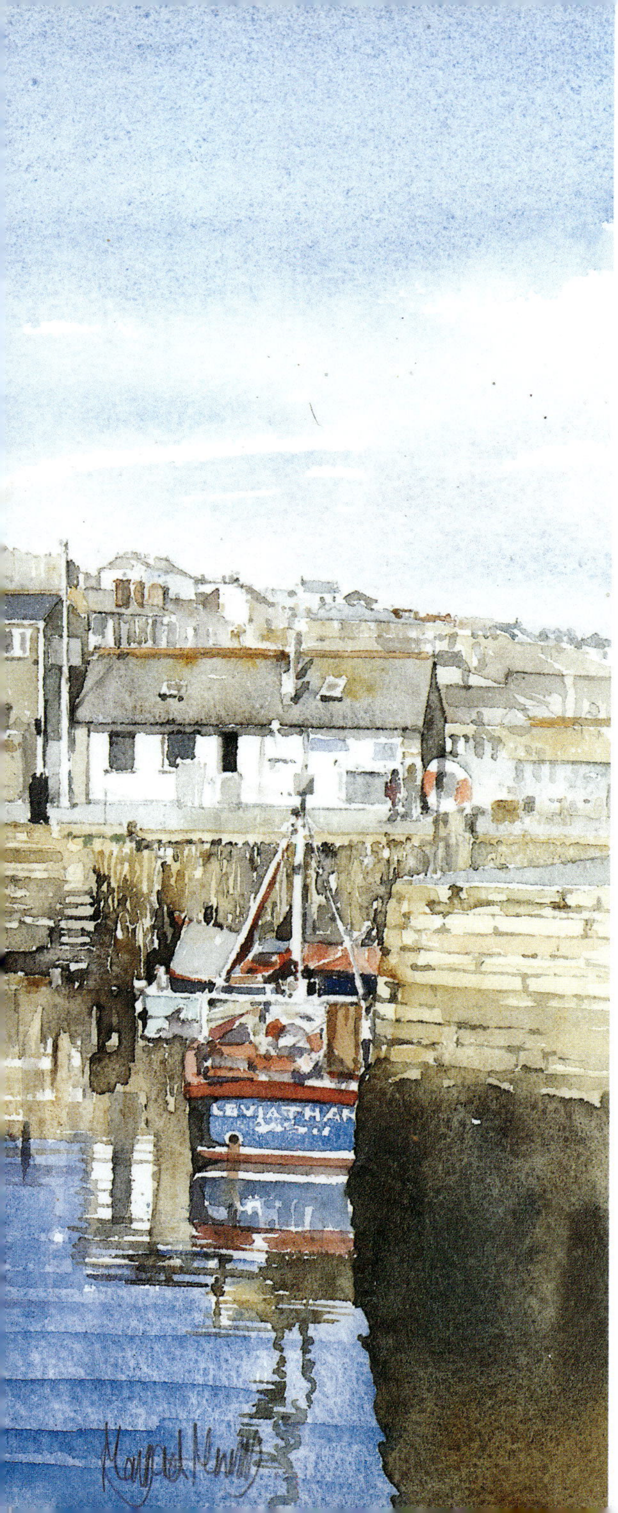

THE RIVER FAL

As an art student, I spent many happy hours perched precariously on the edge of a jetty sketching Custom House Quay. The atmosphere was always particularly exciting on warm summer evenings when visitors thronged and local children dived and swam at high tide among the fishing and pleasure boats. The old waterfront buildings with their weathered textures and haphazard arrangements of chimney pots had particular appeal for me; it is fortunate that not too much of their character has been lost over the years and there is still inspiration to be found.

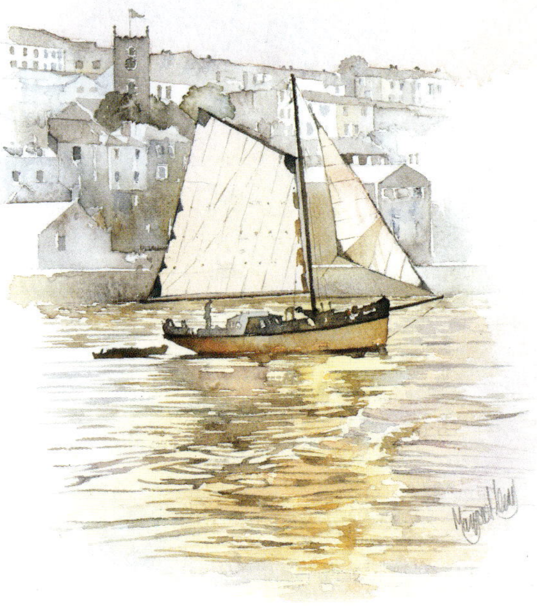

Custom House Quay, Falmouth

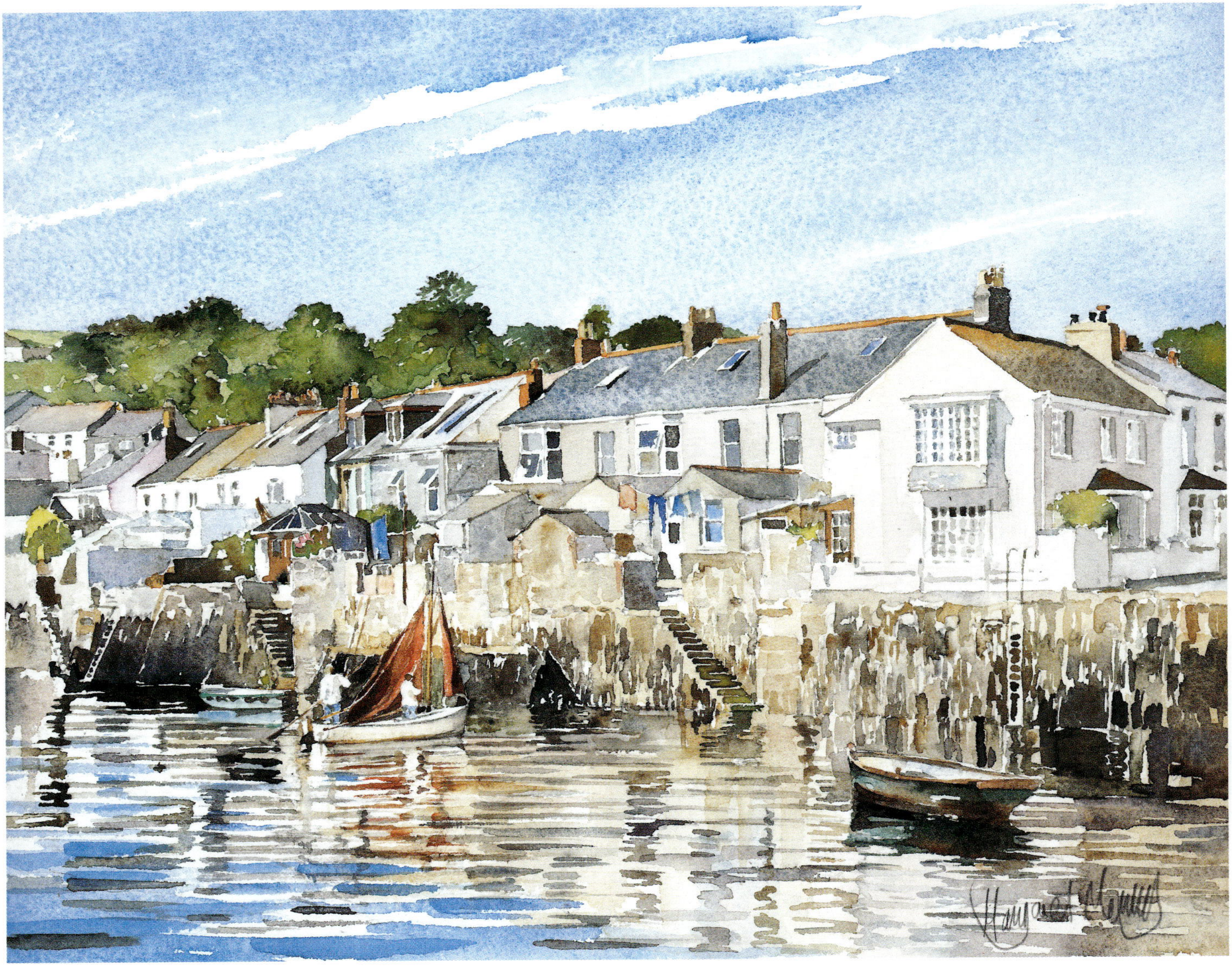

During my Falmouth days, I often used to catch the ferry to Flushing to spend the day on the beach to swim or collect shells. In summer, the narrow streets are hot and sunny and gardens and window boxes are bright with flowers so that it is easy to imagine you are abroad and not in Cornwall at all. There are plenty of painting subjects here and I particularly like the evenings when you can watch the boats returning from their day's sailing and the sun setting over the water.

Not far from King Harry Ferry, with its superb view of Trelissick grounds and mansion, is Turnaware Point, a favourite picnic spot in summer for locals who arrive by boat to spend the day. At this time of year there are always plenty of boats sailing past but for a painting you need a breezy day and a big sky with enough cloud to give a feeling of movement.

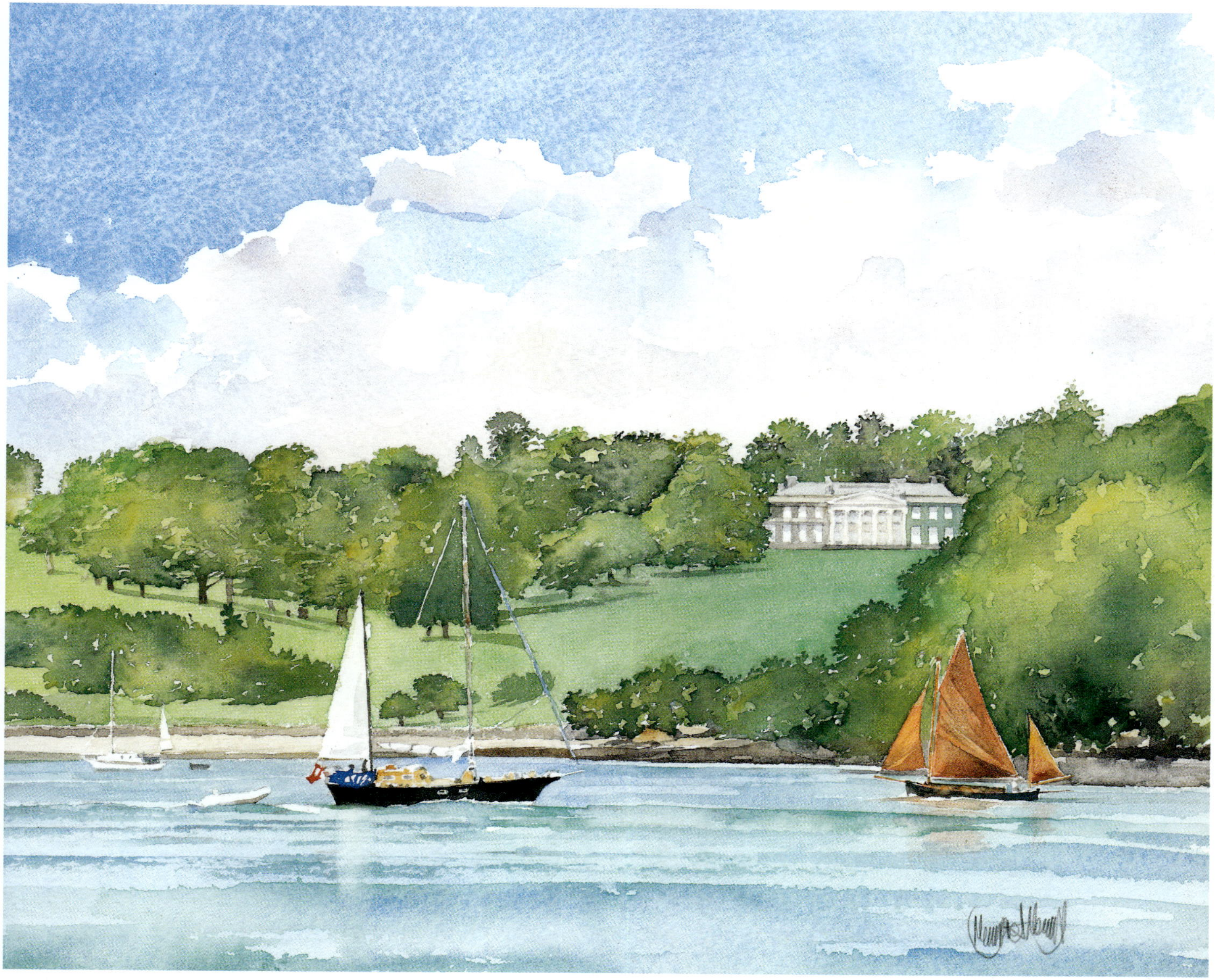

Trelissick from Turnaware Point

This view of the Pandora Inn at Restronguet was painted early in the morning, before the car park filled up. When the tide is in and there is a boat or two in the foreground, as seen here, I think the old thatched buiding, with the trees behind, makes an attractive picture. Swans often swim up to be fed and sometimes a black swan, seen from time to time at various creeks along the river, makes an appearance.

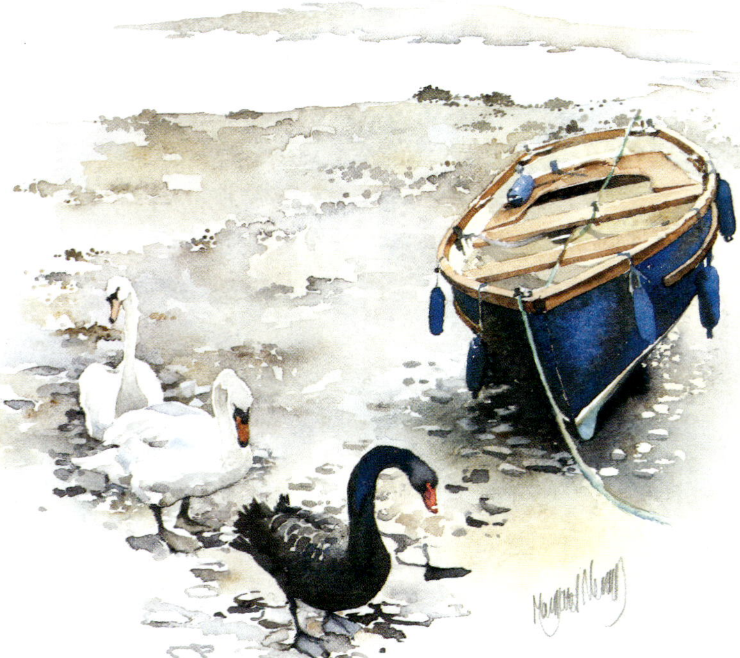

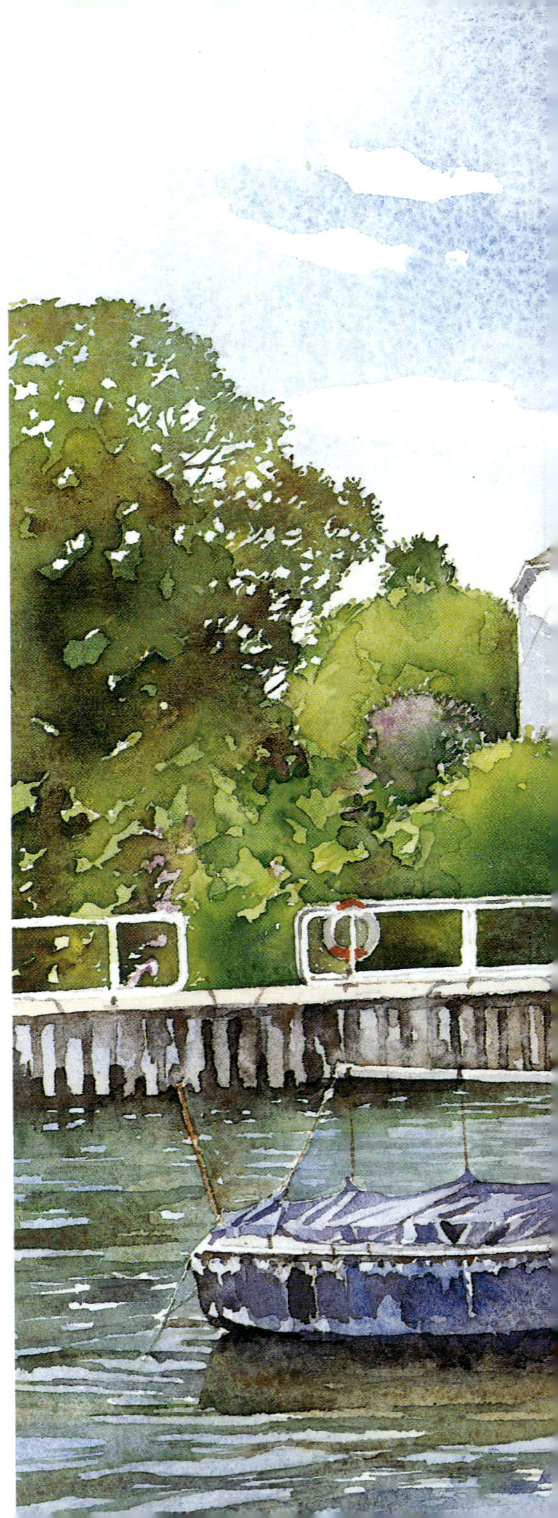

Pandora Inn at Restronguet

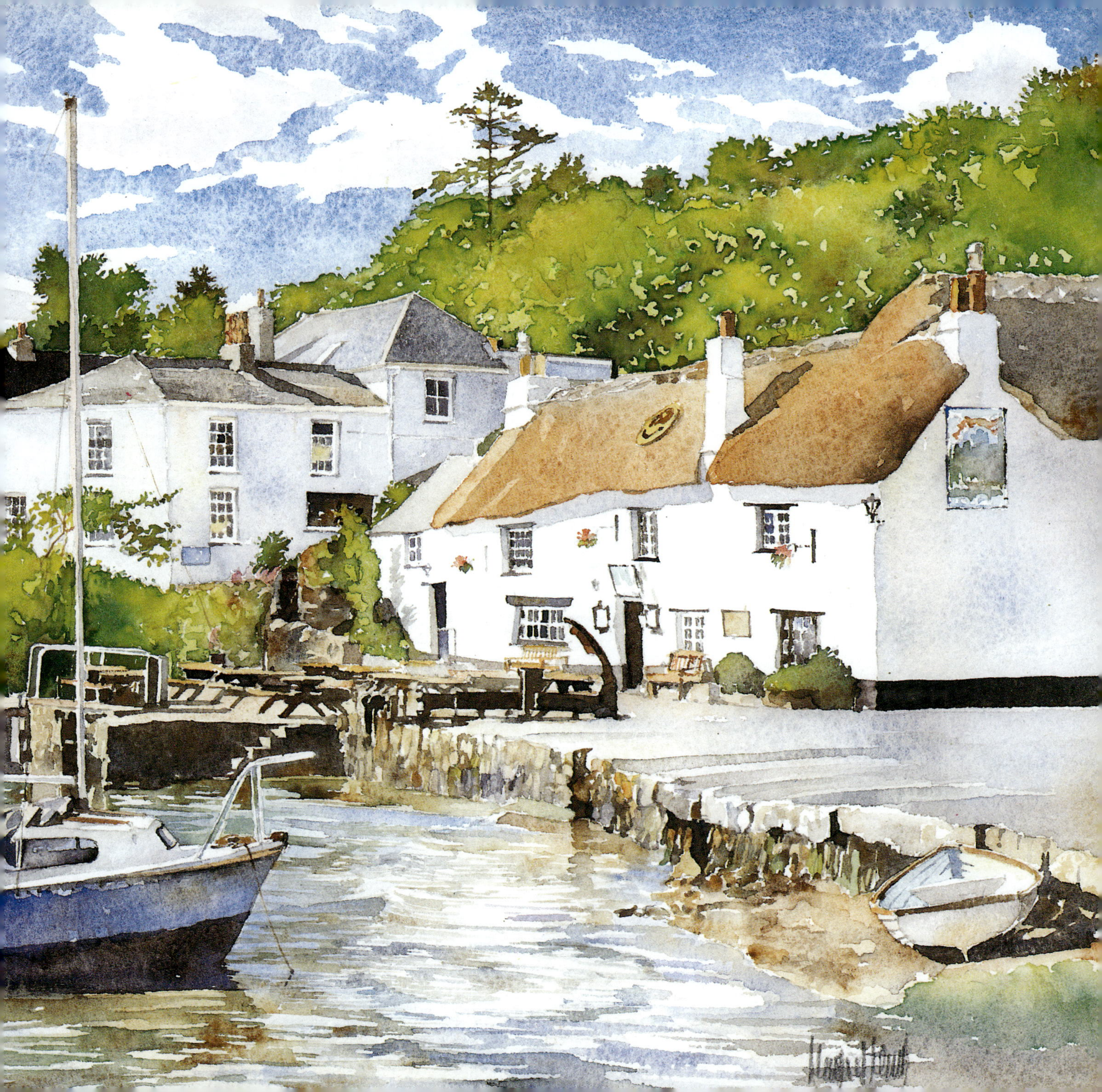

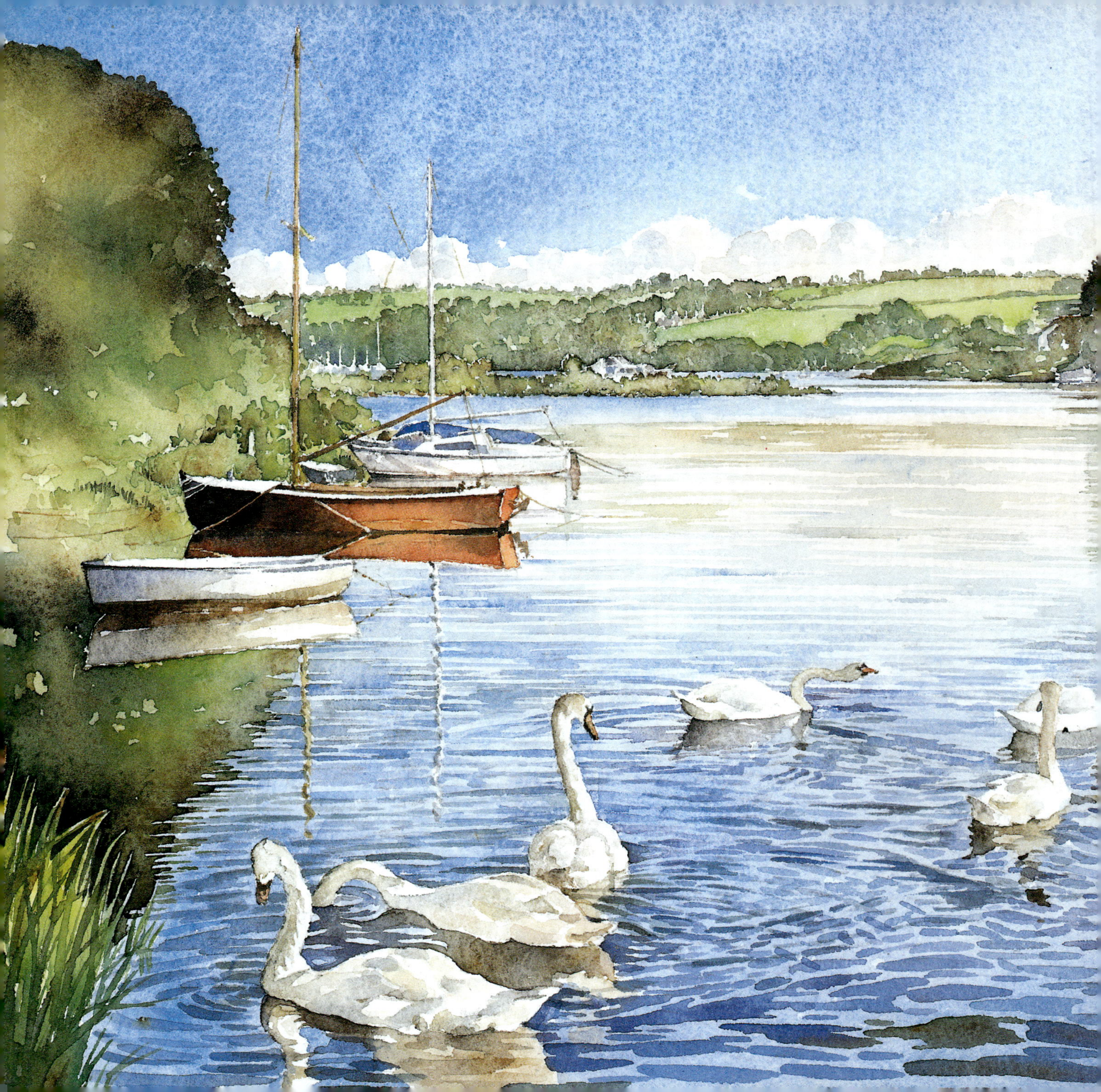

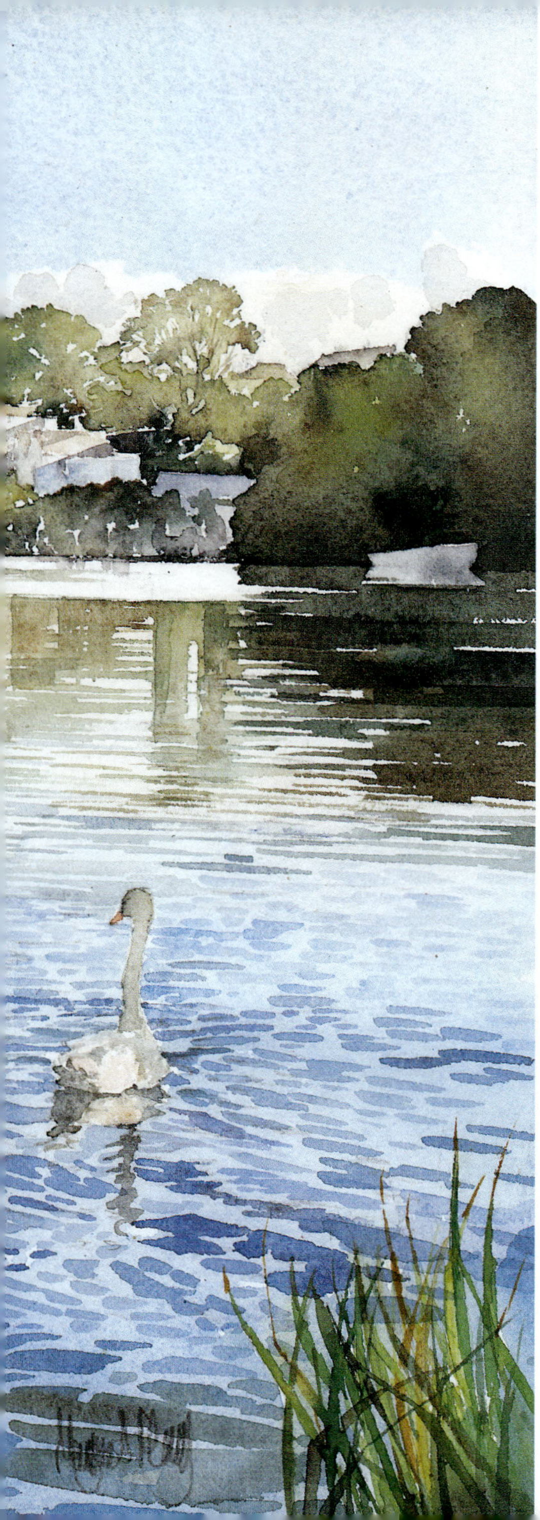

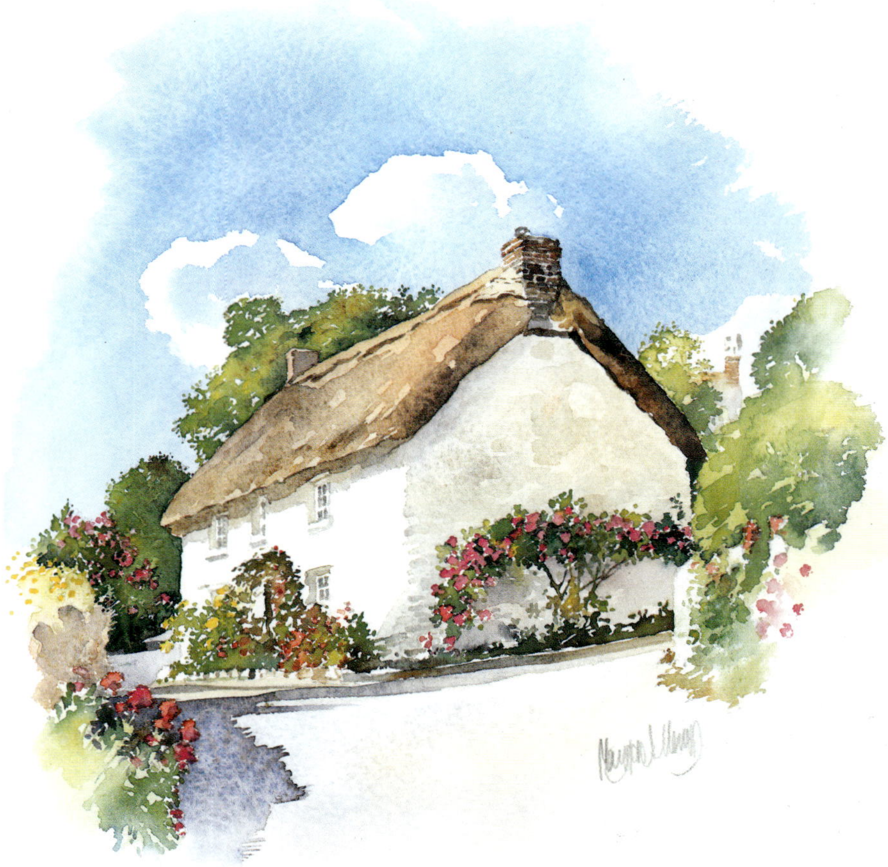

Cottages at Feock

Point has become a sanctuary for swans in recent years, seen here gracing the water at high tide on a summer's evening. At nearby Feock there are more creekside views to paint as well as pretty cottages and a church with an unusual lych-gate.

Point

I used to accompany my father when he went to Coombe every autumn to buy its famous Kea plums for the shop. These days, it is one of my most favourite haunts and I have painted it hundreds of times. This is an Autumn view, but it is equally lovely in Spring, when the blossom is out in the orchards, or on a still, Summer's morning at high tide. The woods and surrounding countryside abound with all kinds of wildlife; at dusk, badgers emerge to follow the little paths made by previous generations of badgers on their nightly forays while on the opposite bank, free from human disturbance, mallards and shelducks rear their young.

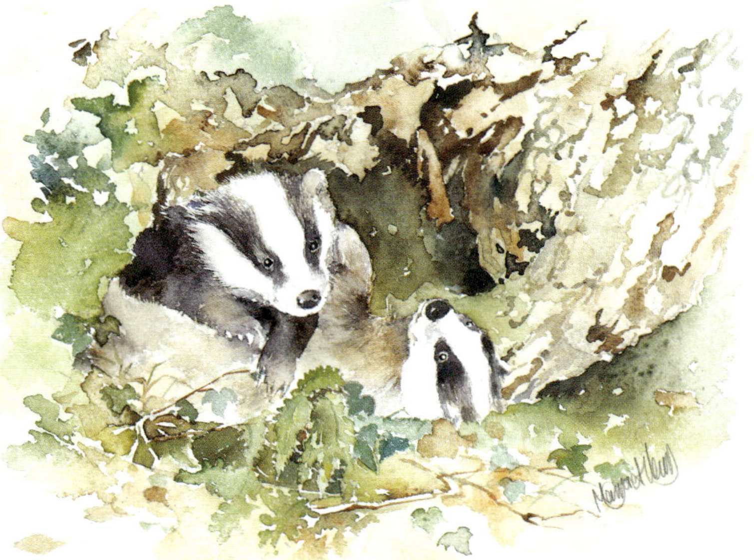

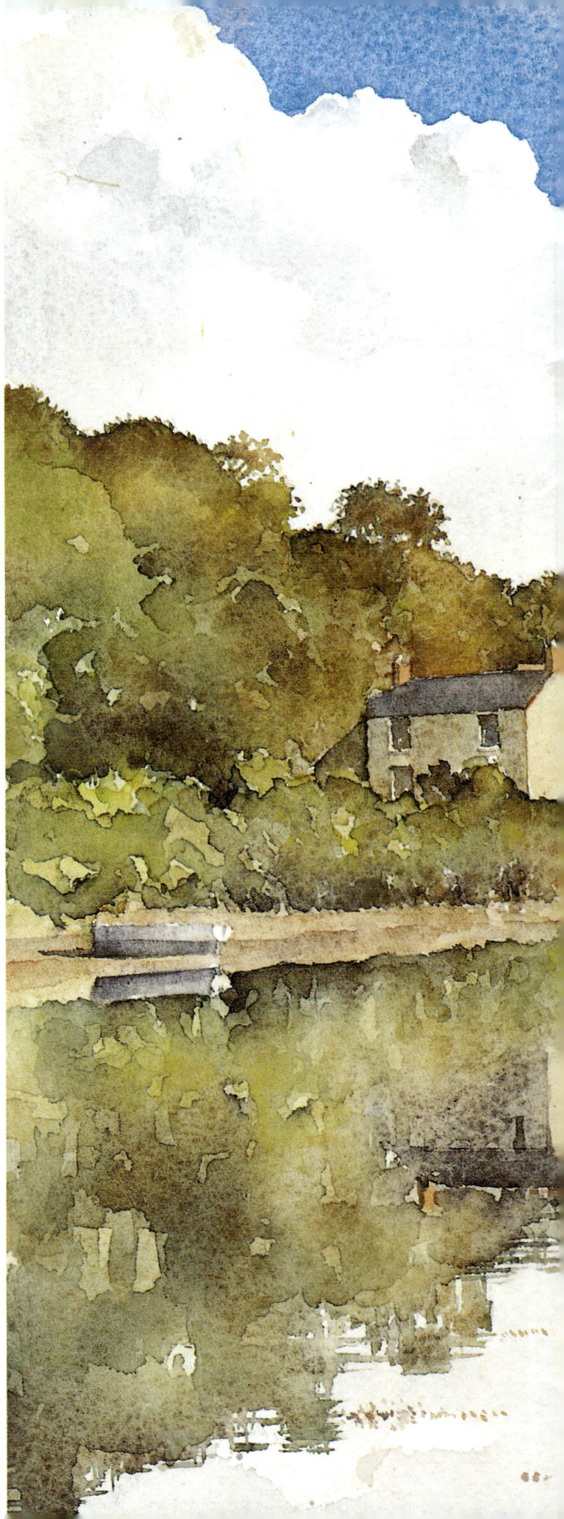

Coombe Creek

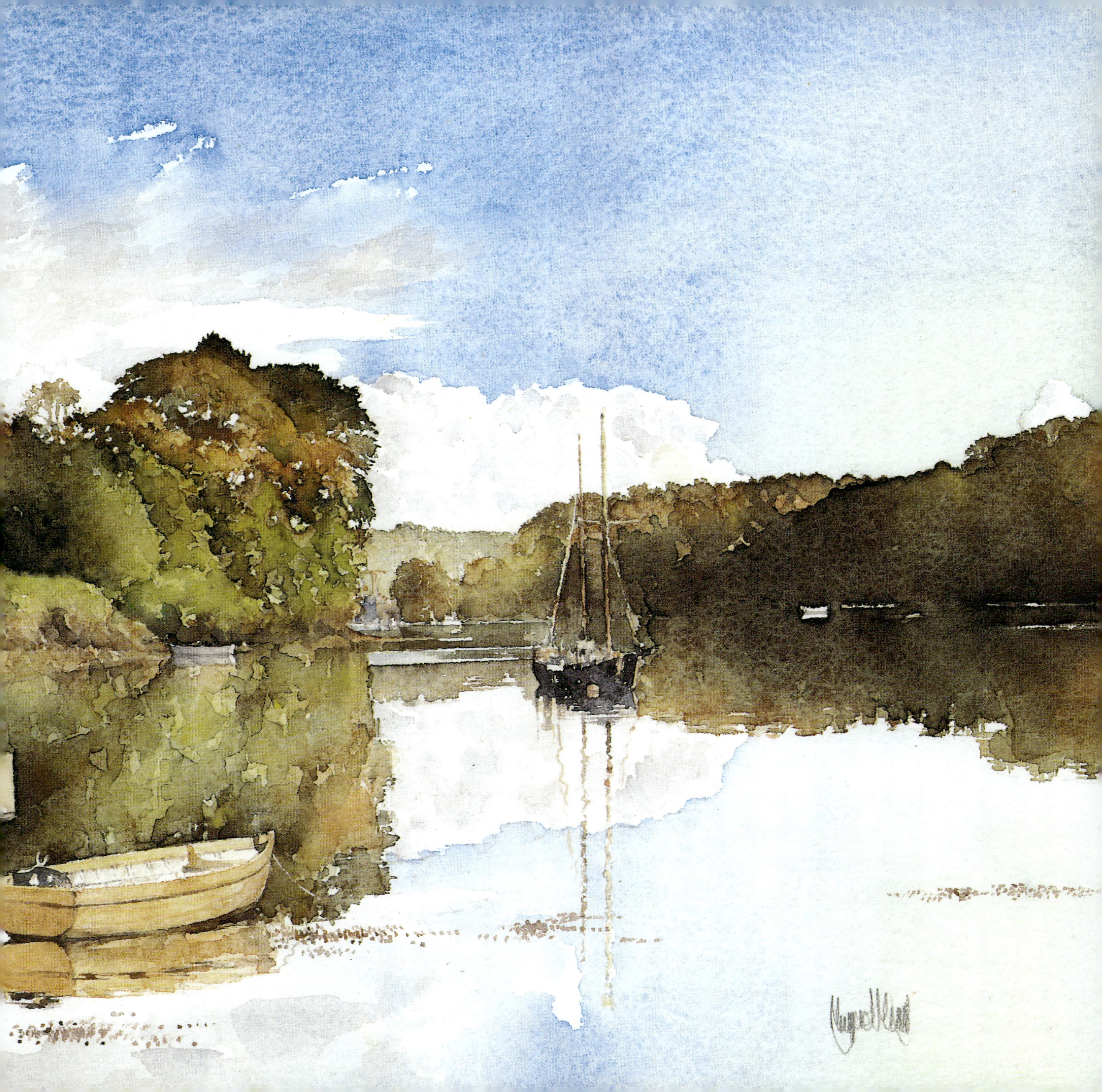

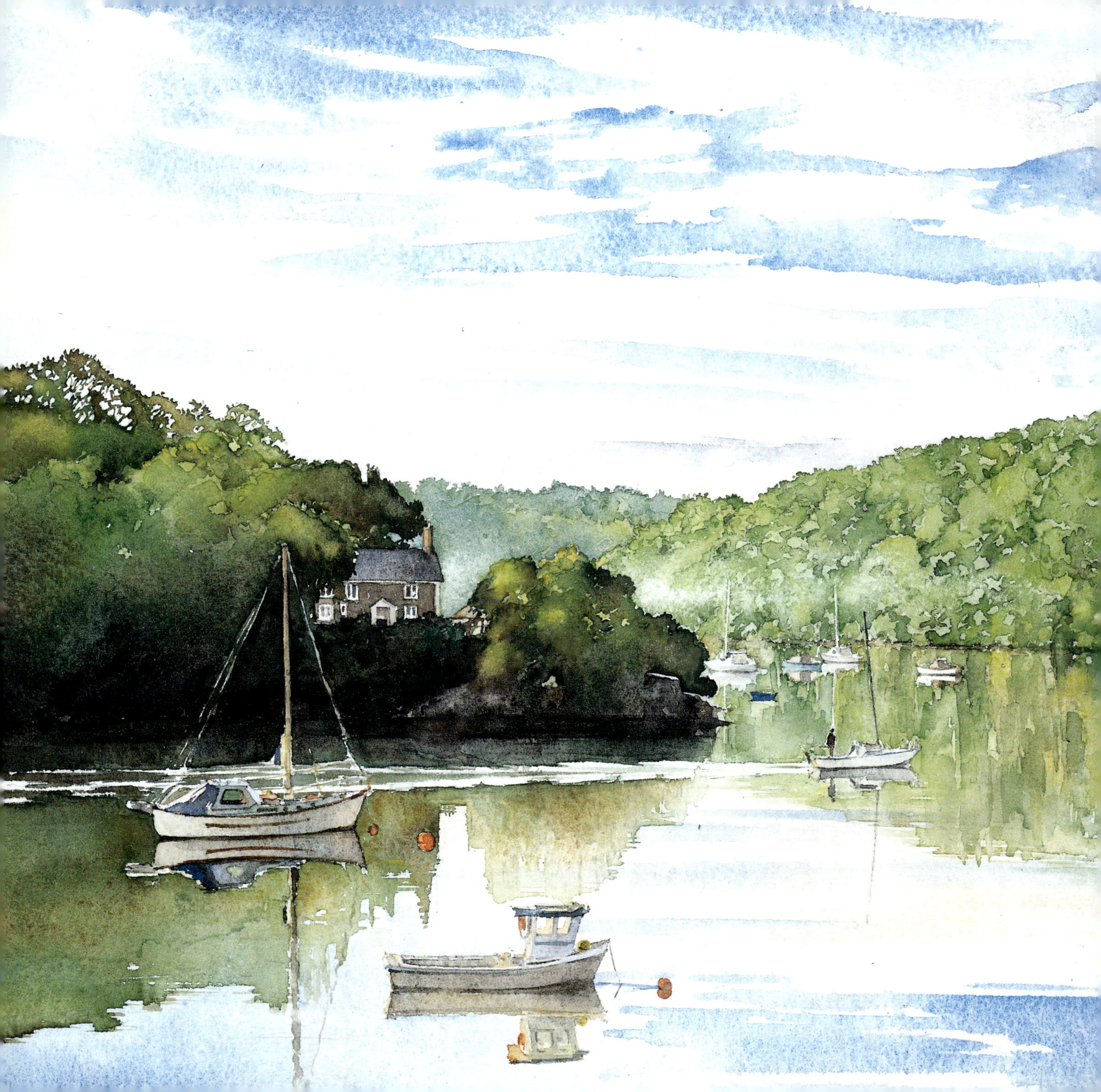

THE TRURO RIVER

At high tide, early on a fine morning while the light is still soft and before the wind has got up to ruffle the glassy reflections, there is no finer or more romantic view of the river than this one of the ferryman's cottage at Malpas.

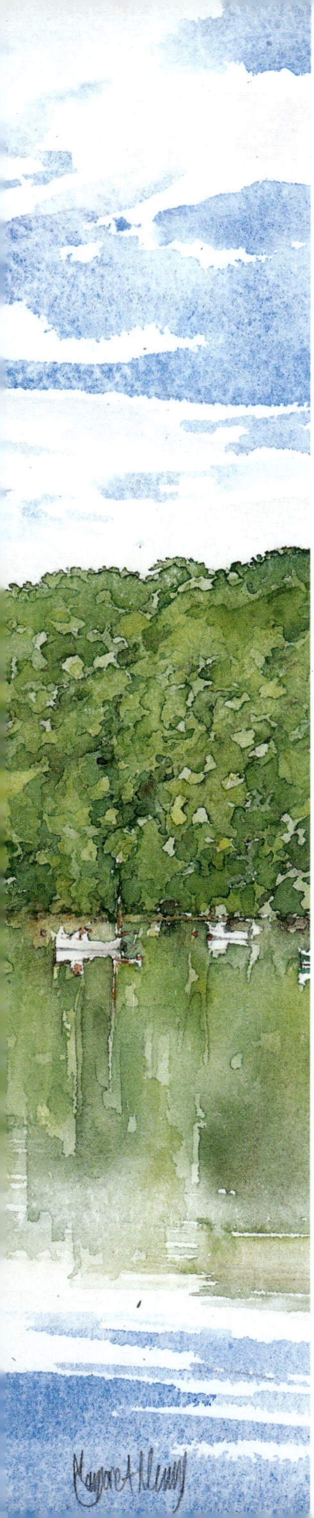

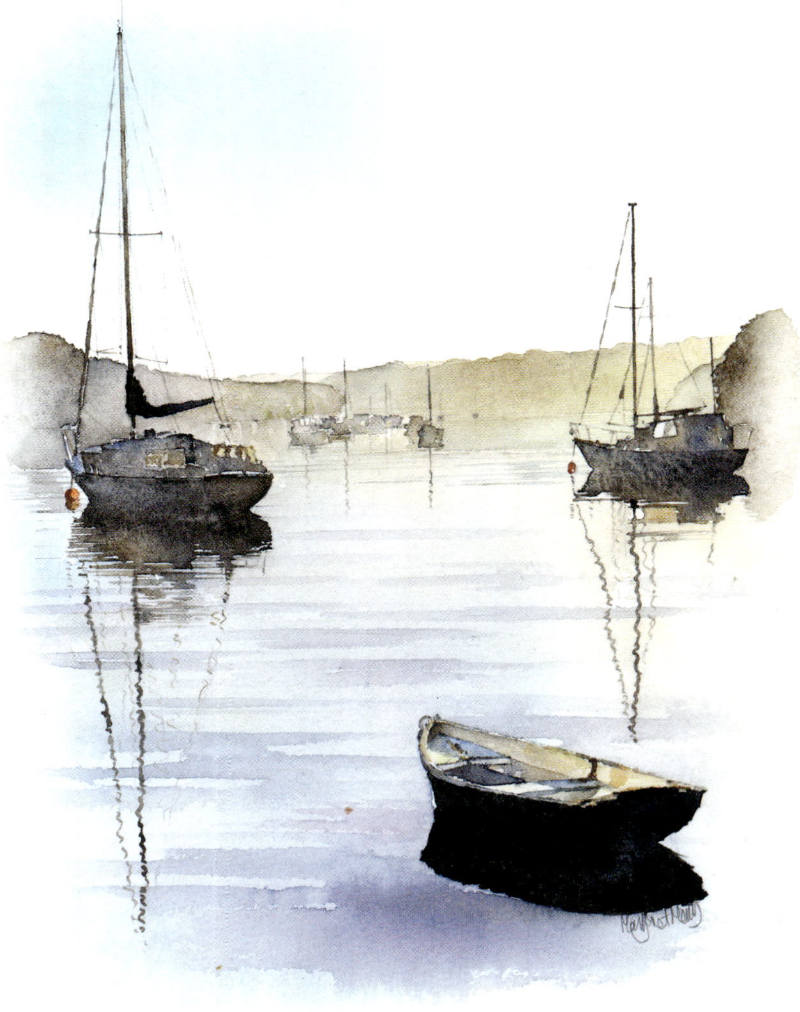

Malpas

Hideous, modern structures have replaced many of the lovely, old, waterfront buildings which I so loved to draw and paint when I first came to live in Truro. These are a few of the remaining ones, painted here in pastel.

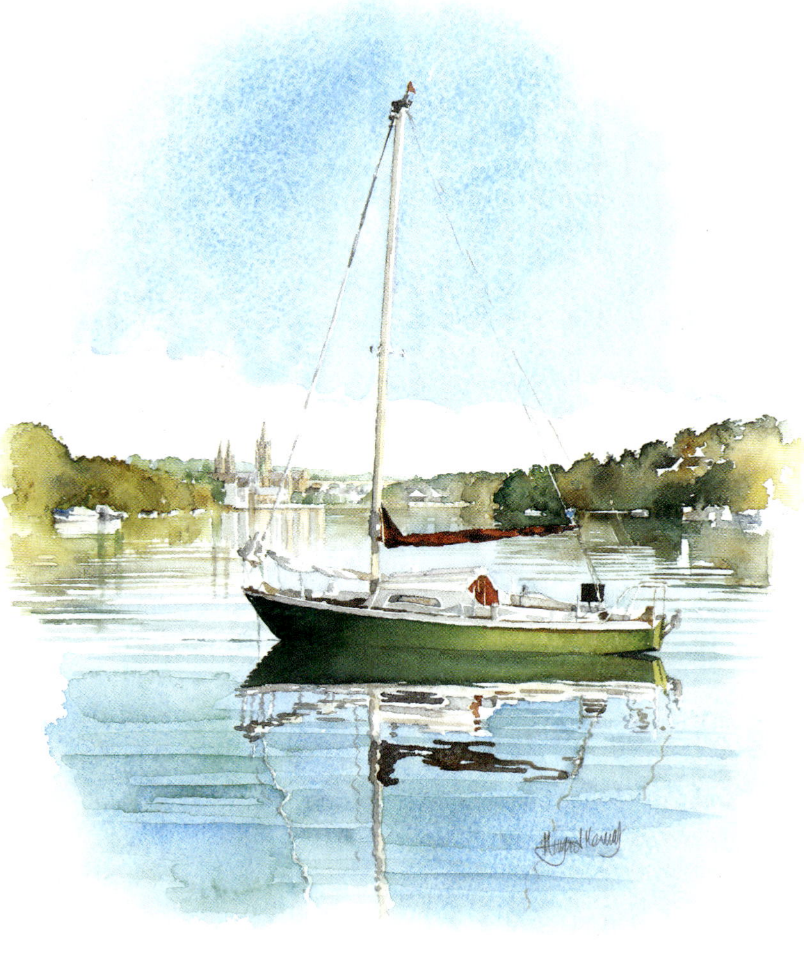

The river at Truro

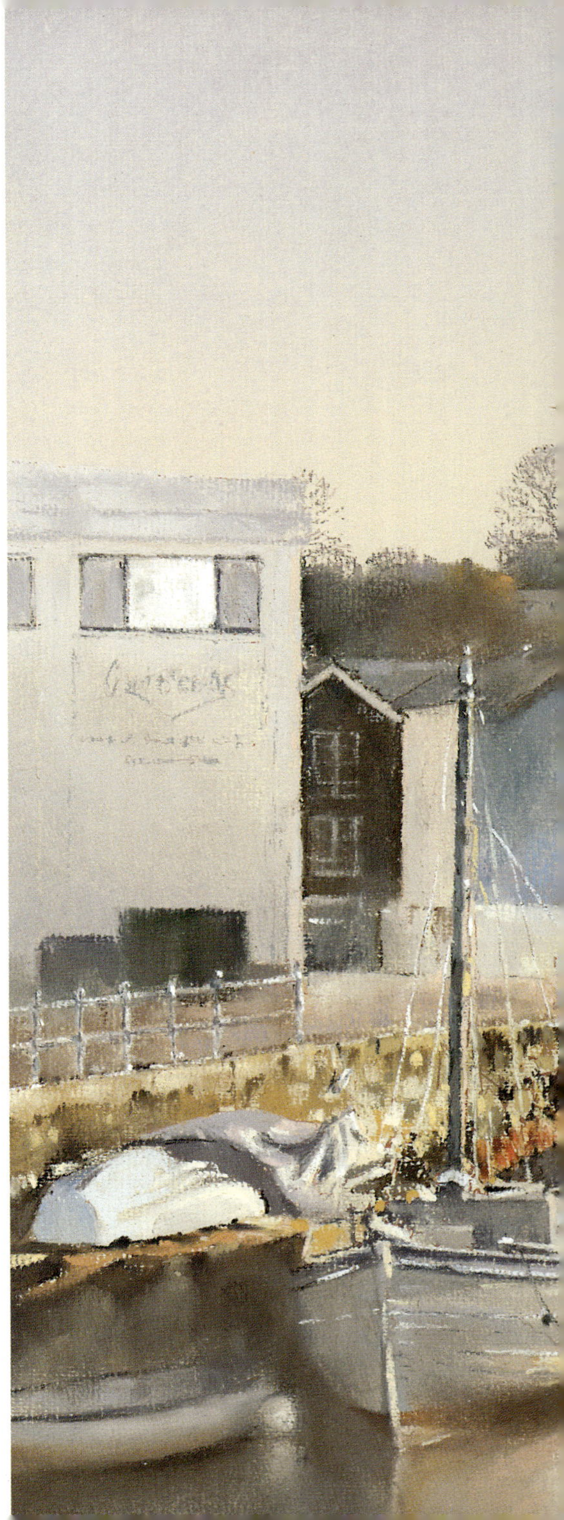

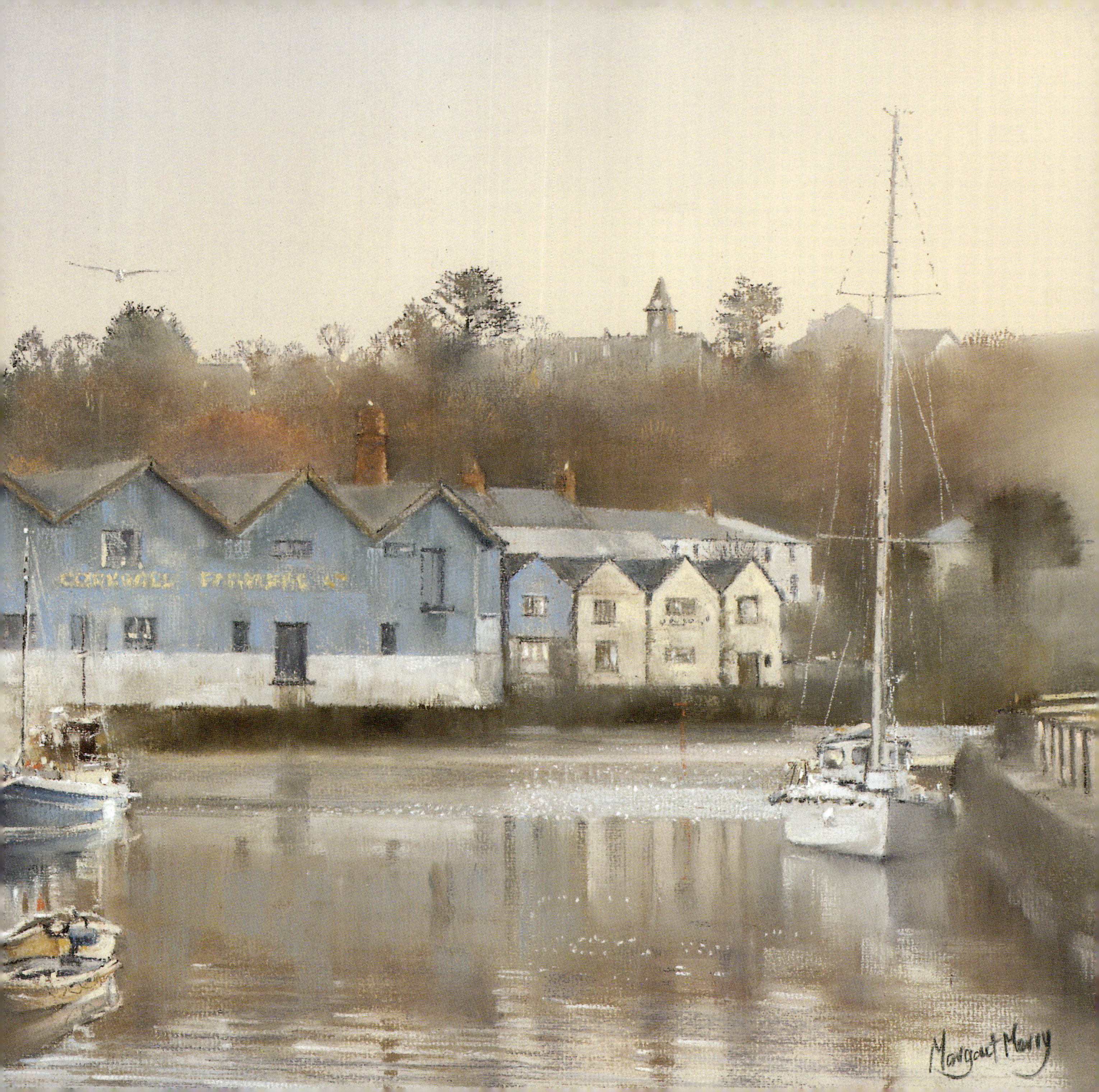
Margaret Merry

How beautiful it must have been, fifty years ago, to walk along the river path at St. Clement at night with the way illuminated by glow-worms in their myriads! Modern farming practices have done their worst and disease has destroyed the canopy of elms. But the river is still lovely and pastel is the perfect medium for capturing the early morning light at high tide, as I have tried to do here.

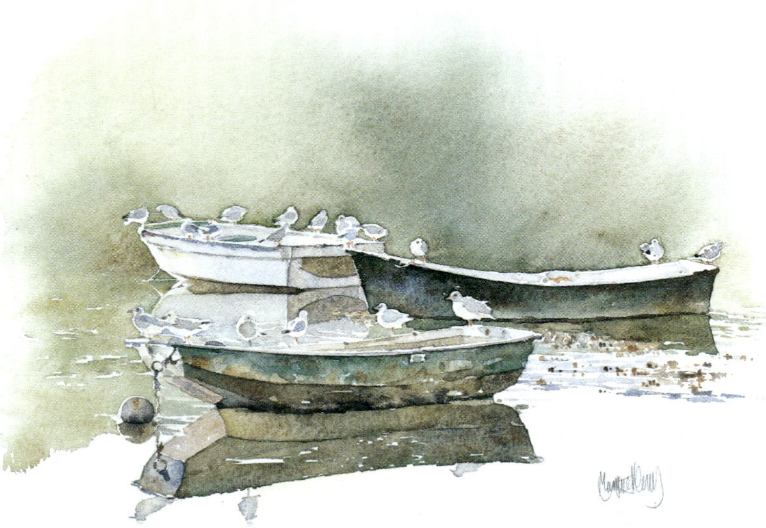

St. Clement

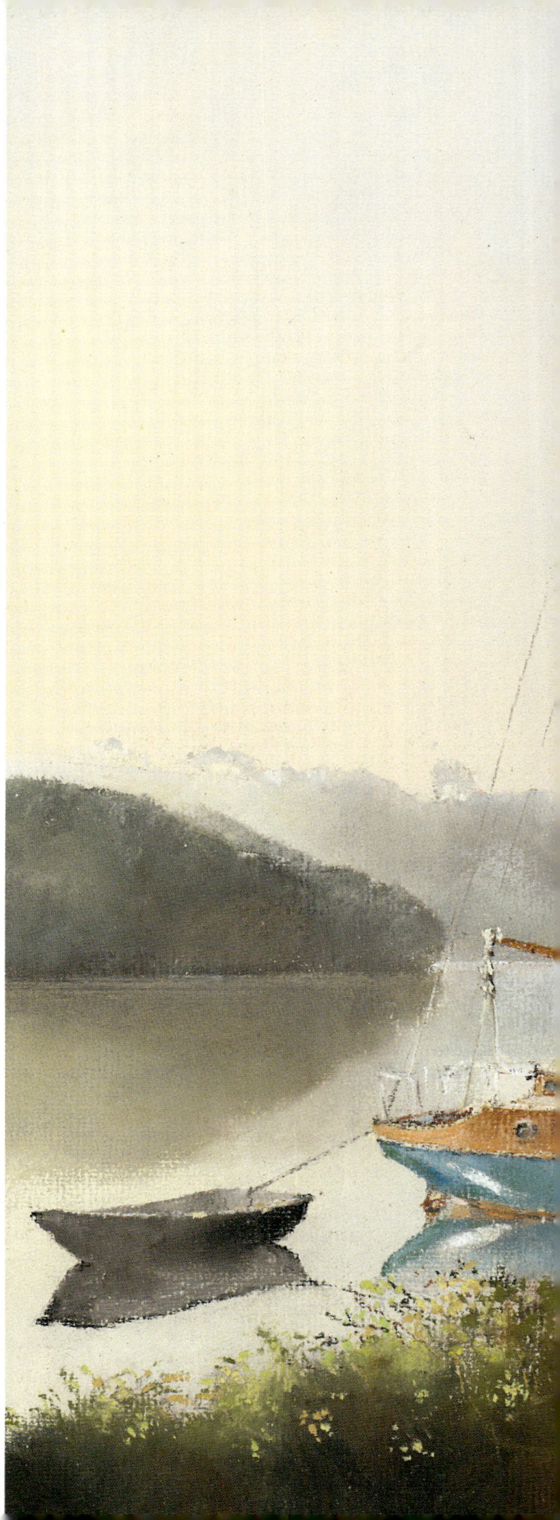

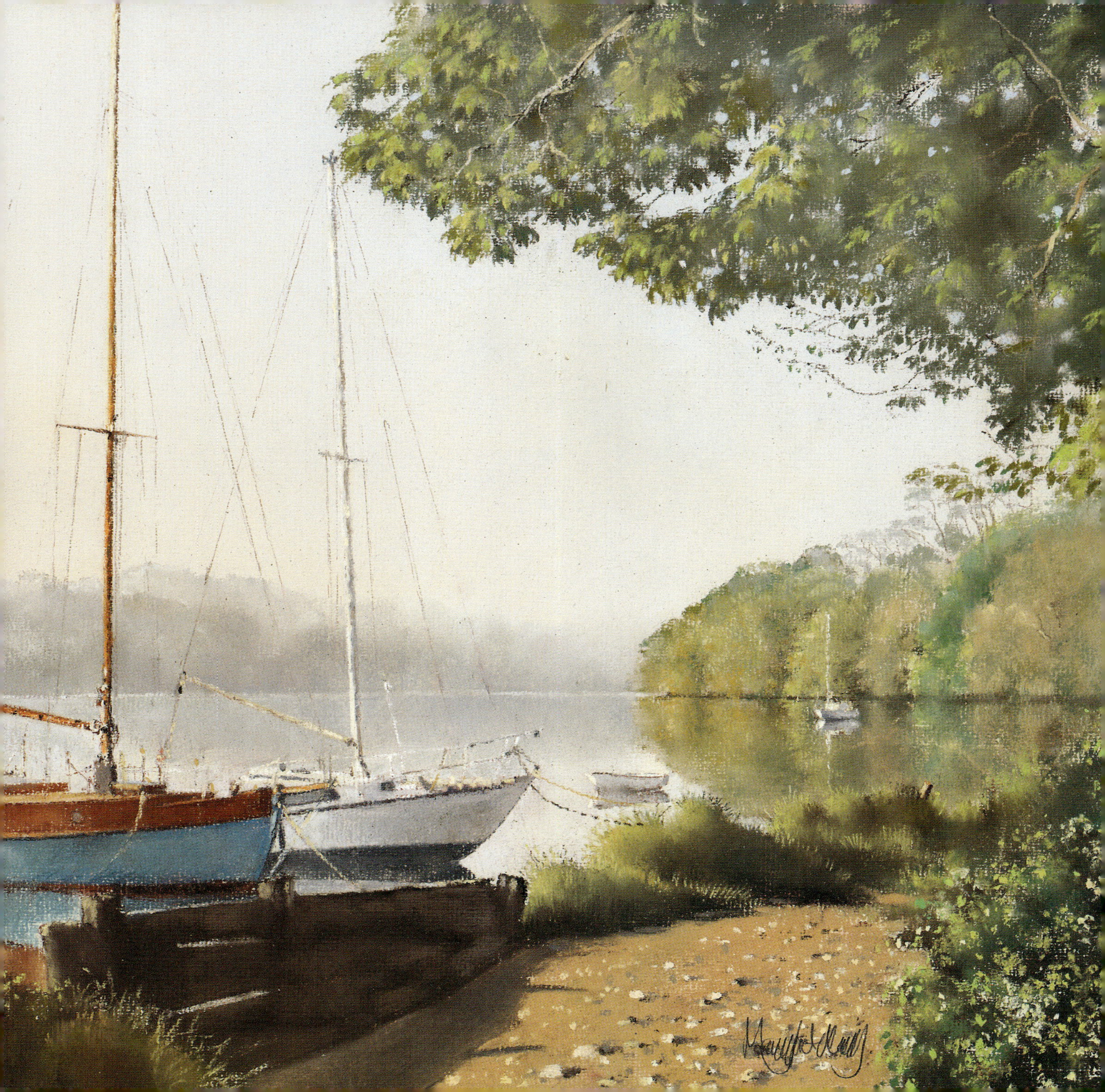

The Tresillian river is famous for the birdlife it supports and halfway between St. Clement and Pencalenick, at Tresemple Pond, birdwatchers are often seen. Herons are commonplace, as are the once rare visitors from southern Europe, but now resident, little egrets. If you are patient, you can generally see a kingfisher; this pair of handsome Canada geese are occasional visitors.

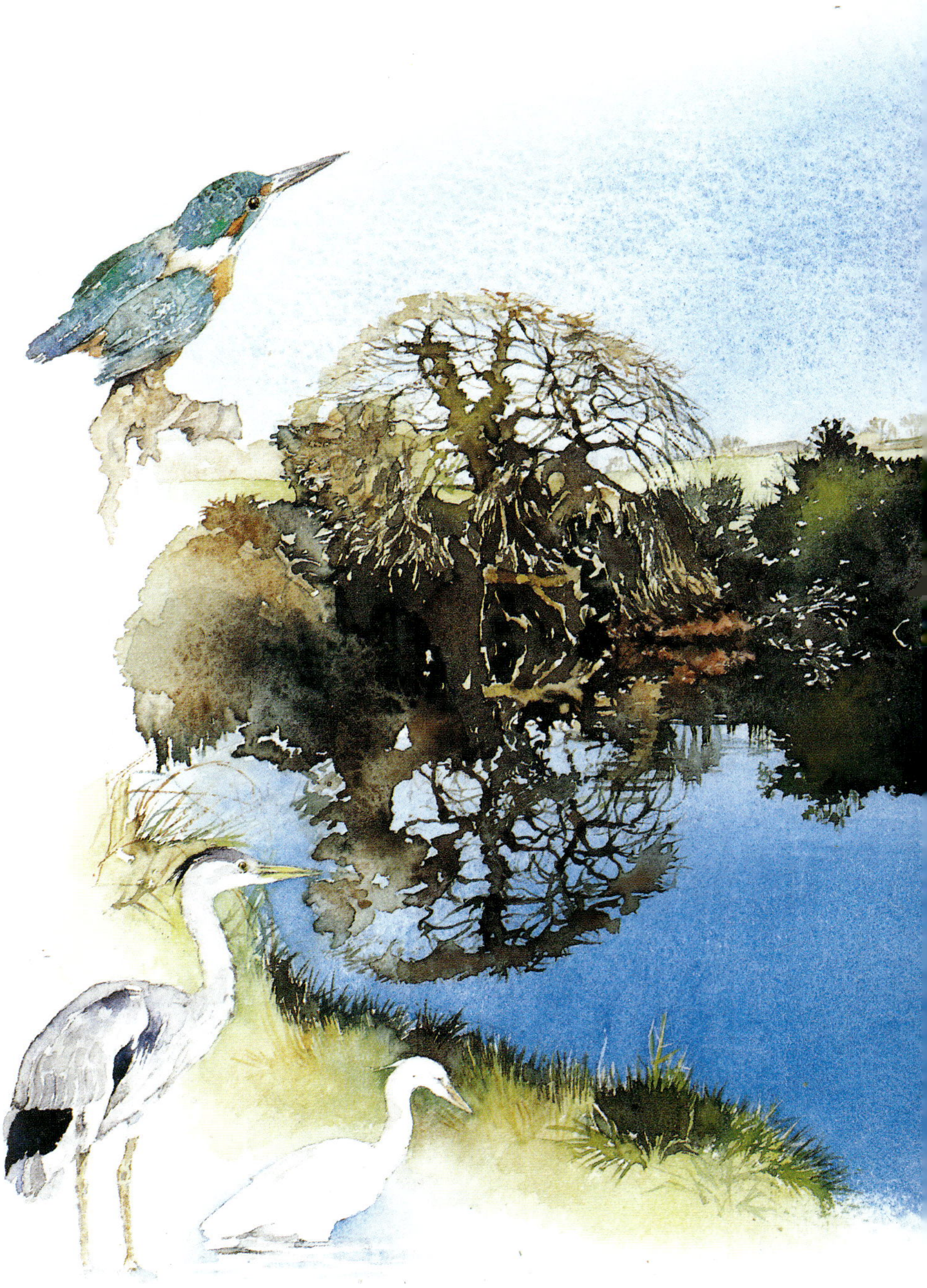

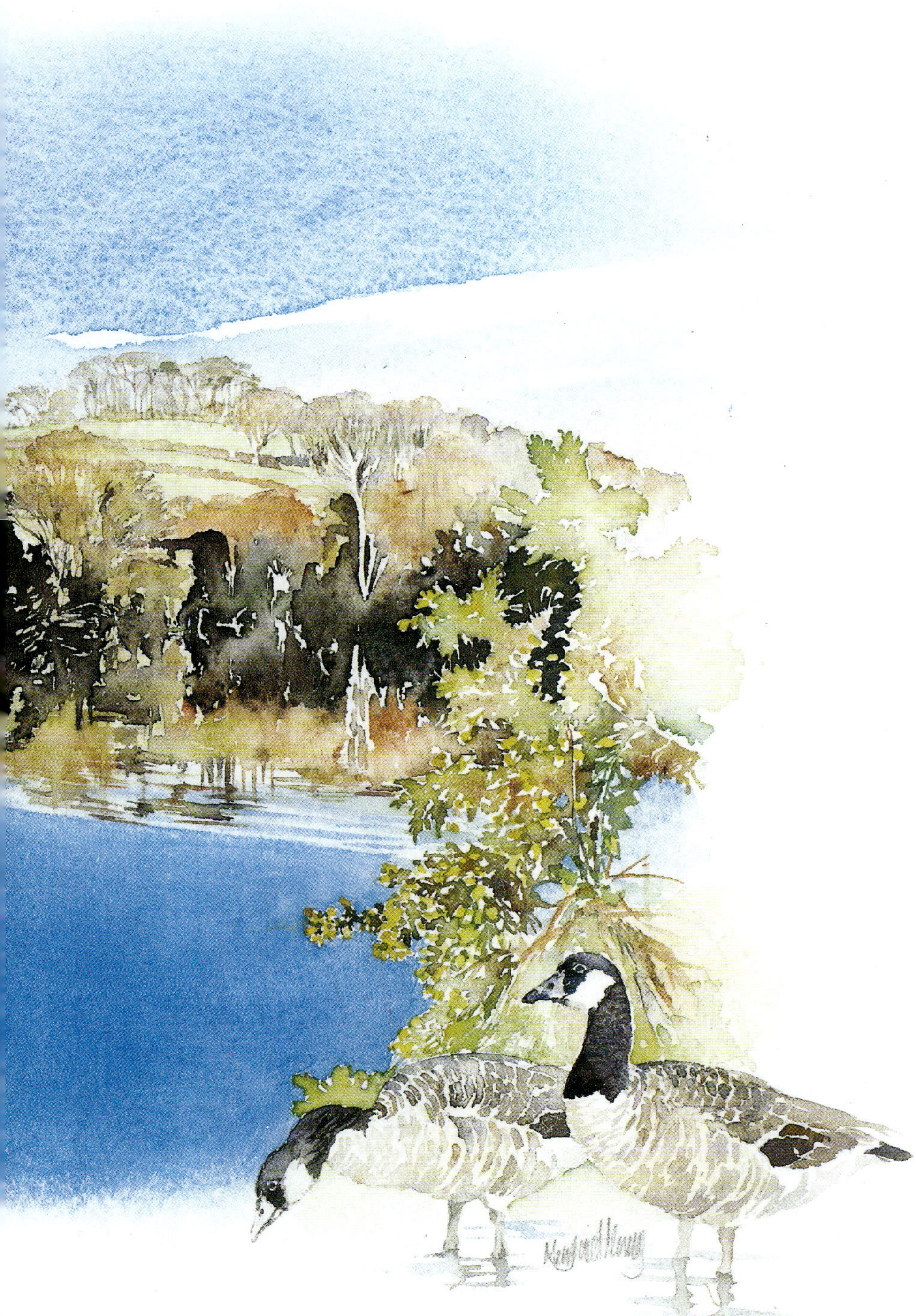

Tresemple pond between St.Clement and Tresillian

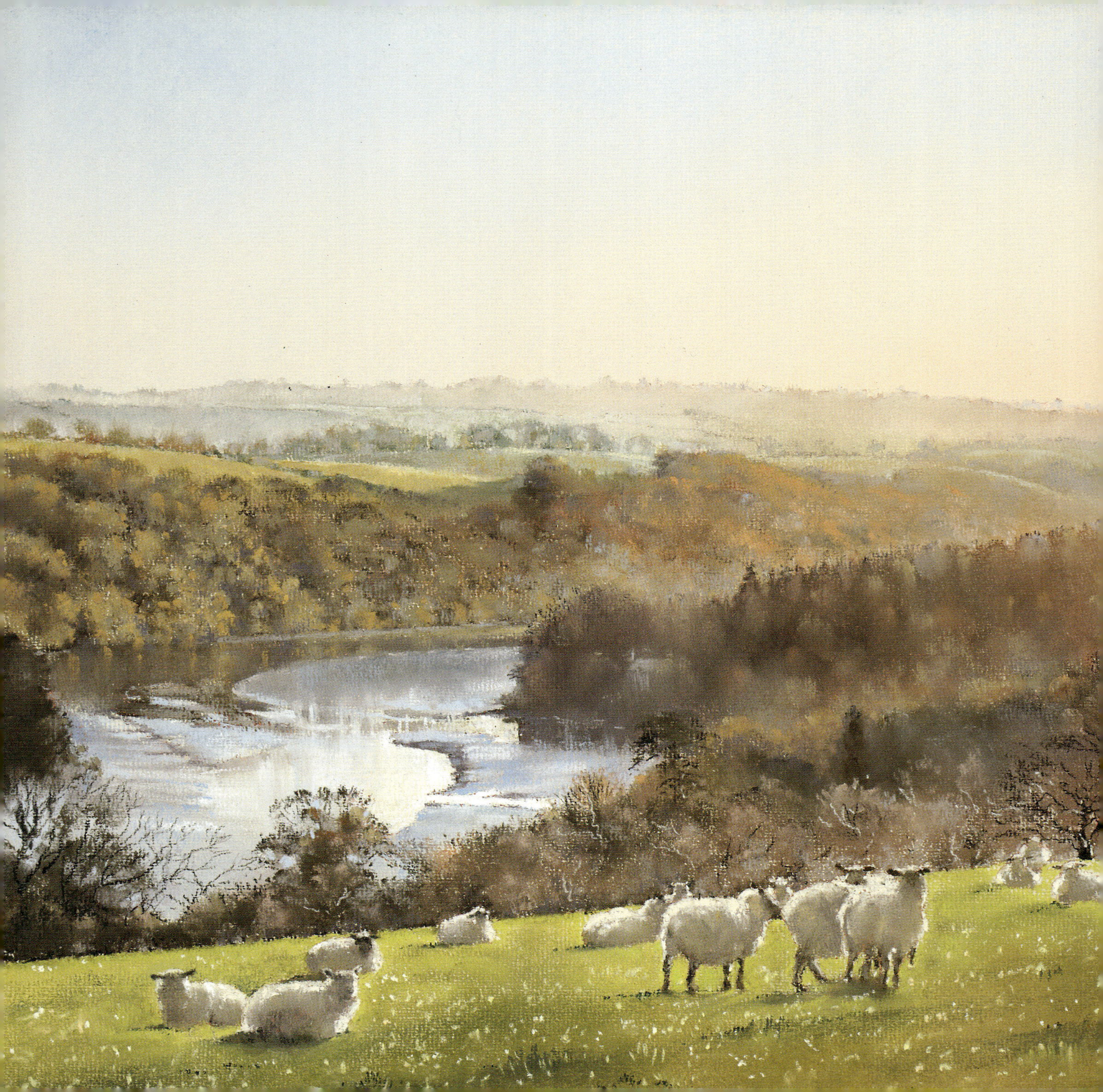

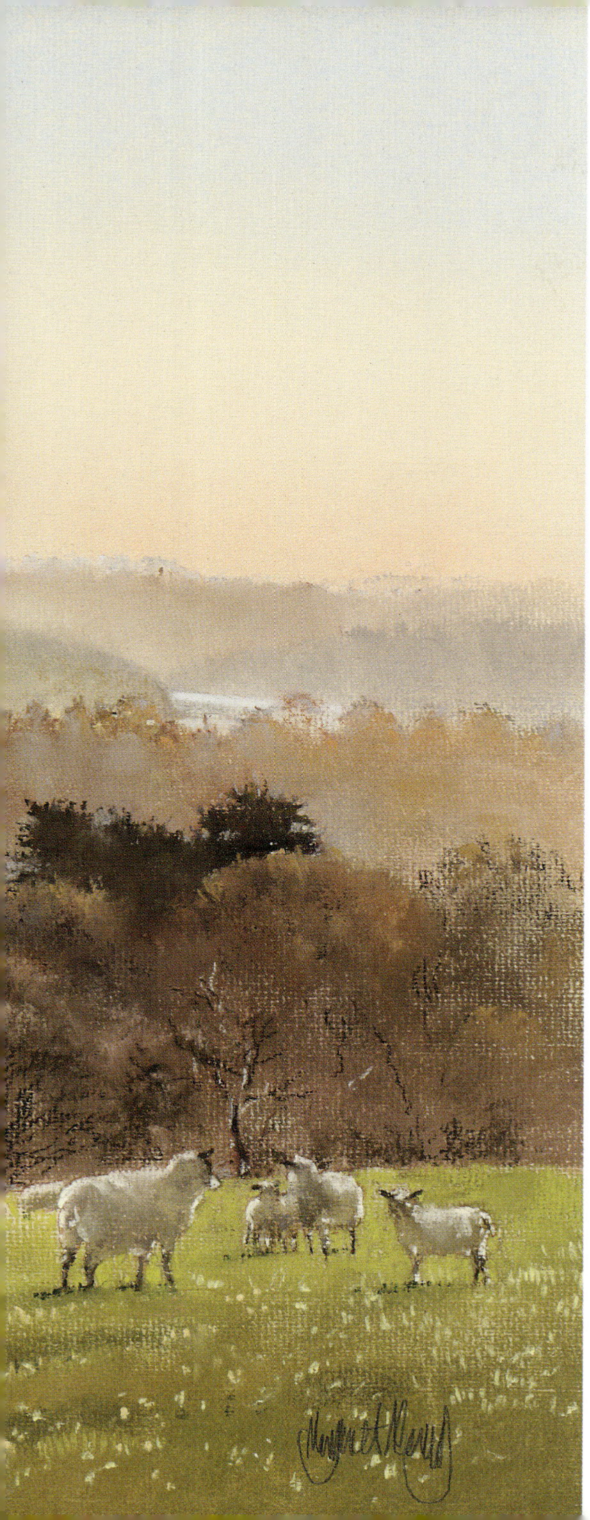

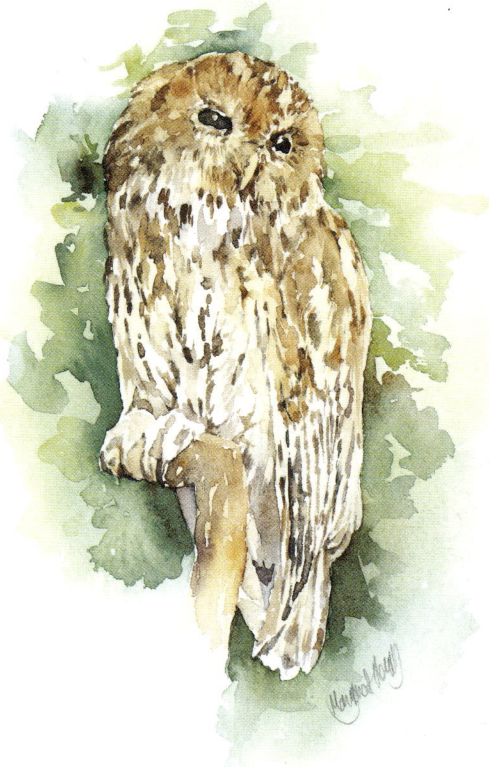

This view of the Tresillian river literally does take your breath away as it is seen from the top of a very steep field. I painted it on a beautiful afternoon in January and I used pastel in order to capture the delicate pinkness of the sky, the reflection of the sun on the water and the light falling on the fleeces of the sheep in the foreground.

In winter, even before nightfall, tawny owls begin to call from the woods and not infrequently, in the dead of night, you hear the melancholy cry of a solitary curlew.

ROSELAND

Bridges make interesting subjects for paintings and this, Sett Bridge at Ruan Lanihorne, is particularly attractive. It was not all that long ago that boats could sail up to the village but now most of the waterway is silted up. At dusk, it is a great thrill to see barn owls flying low and silently seeking out small mammals which abound in reedy places such as these.

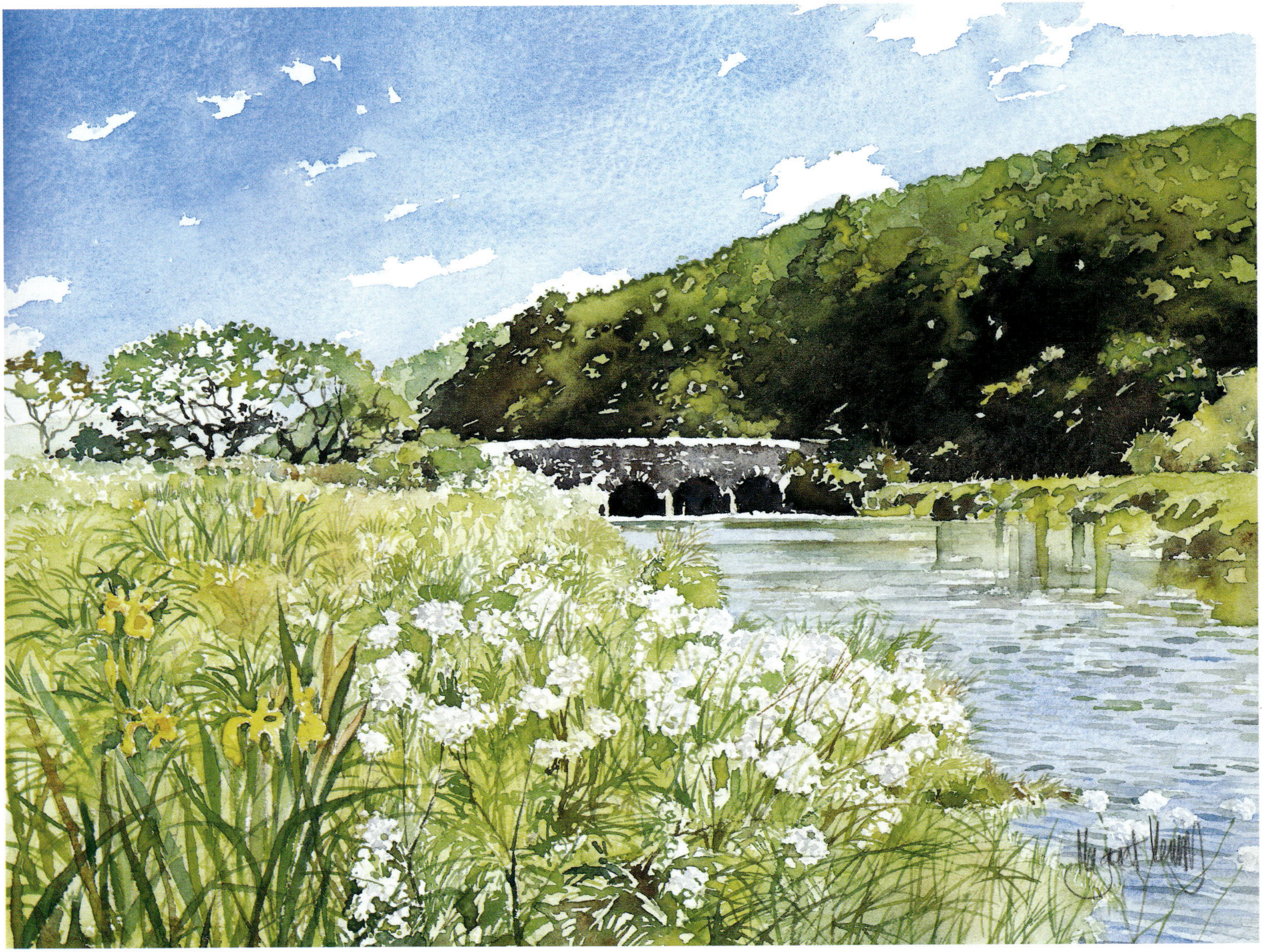

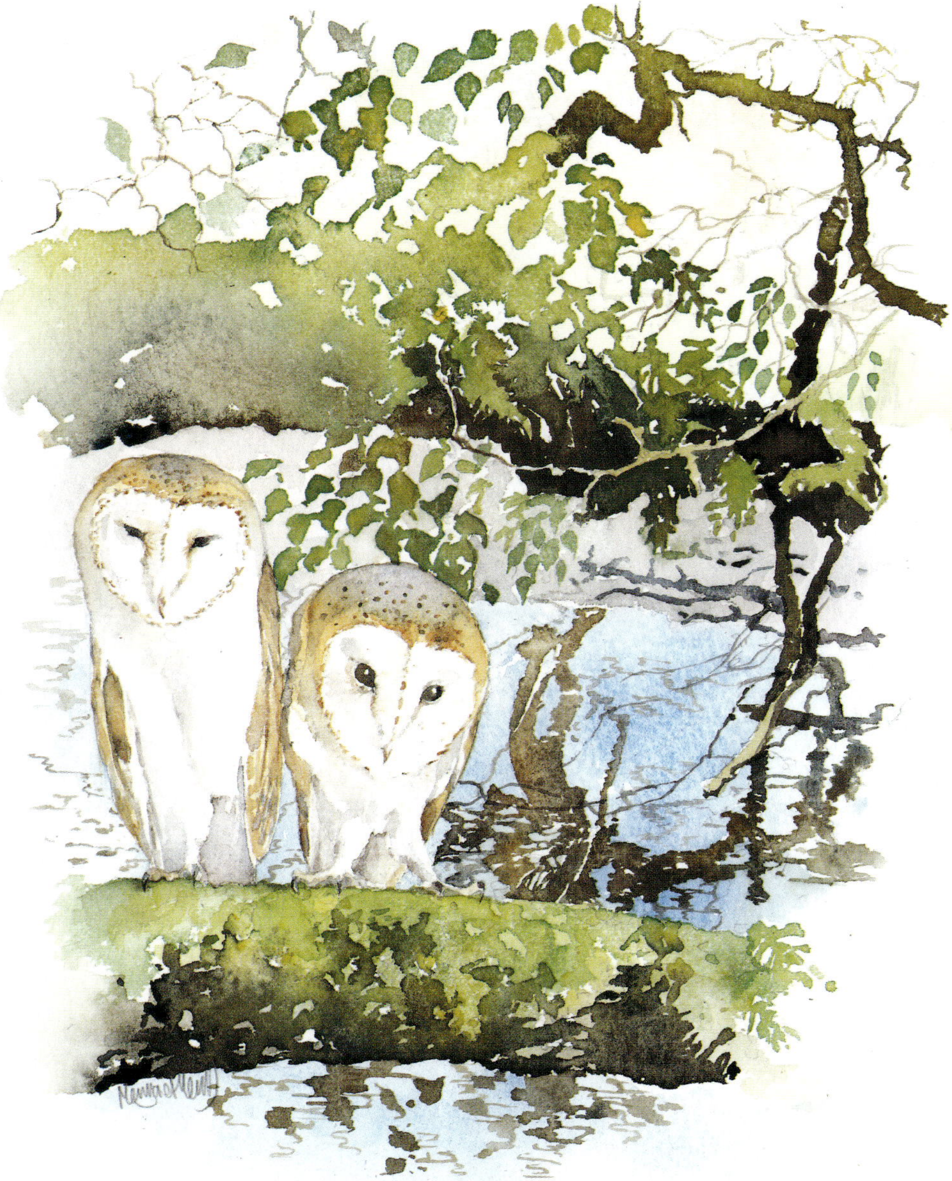

Sett Bridge at Ruan Lanihorne

In winter, Portscatho seems to me to have the rather forlorn and deserted atmosphere that is typical of some Cornish harbour resorts. But on a bright and breezy afternoon in August it is a very different story: scudding clouds, turquoise water and brightly painted boats contrive to make a scene which is full of light and colour.

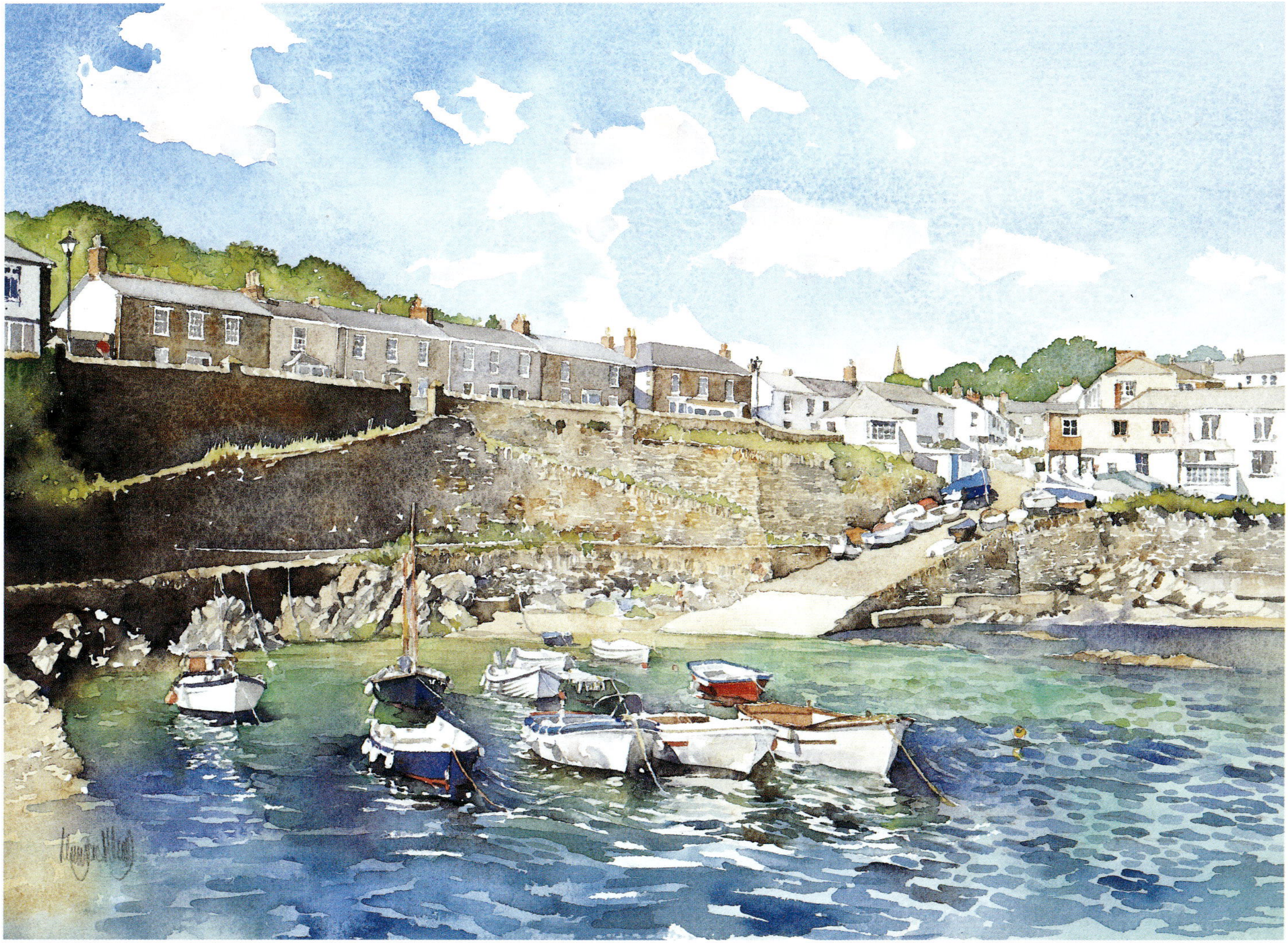

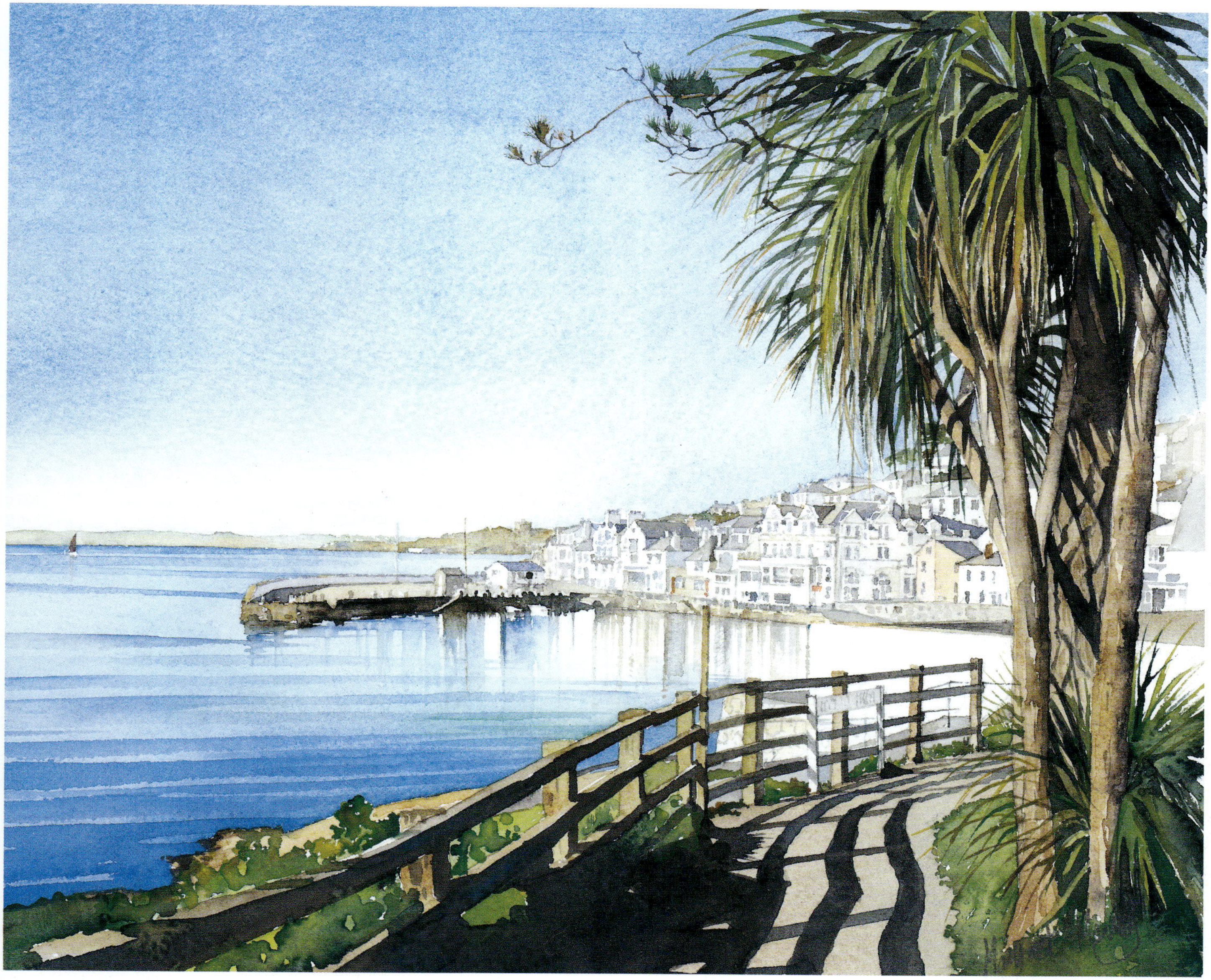

St. Mawes

This is the view you are presented with as you round the bend to begin the descent into St.Mawes and on a fine day, with sunlight reflected on the white buildings and sparkling on the transparent water, you could easily imagine yourself to be on the Continent. I liked this composition with the trees in the foreground and the shadows of the fence on the pavement in the low morning sunshine.

I think St. Just in Roseland deserves its reputation of having the most beautiful churchyard on earth, despite the loss, in a hurricane, of so many of the sheltering pines which were so much a feature of the location. Here, I have tried to capture a mood of tranquility and seclusion and I have framed the composition with overhanging branches to compensate for the missing trees.

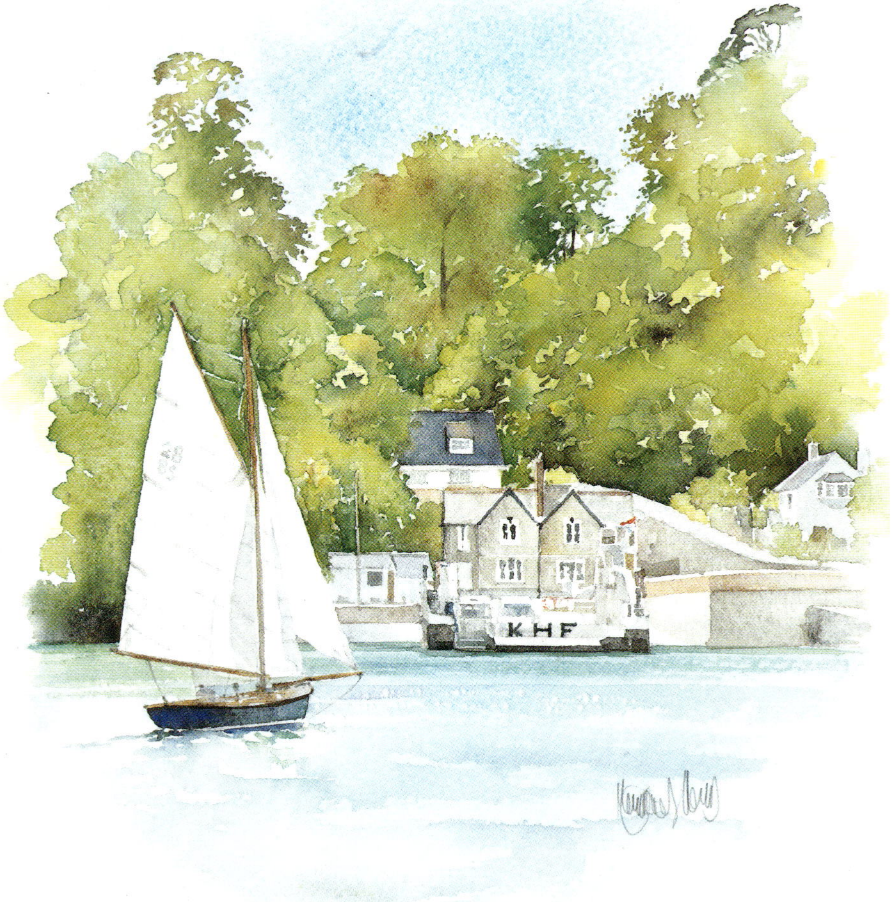

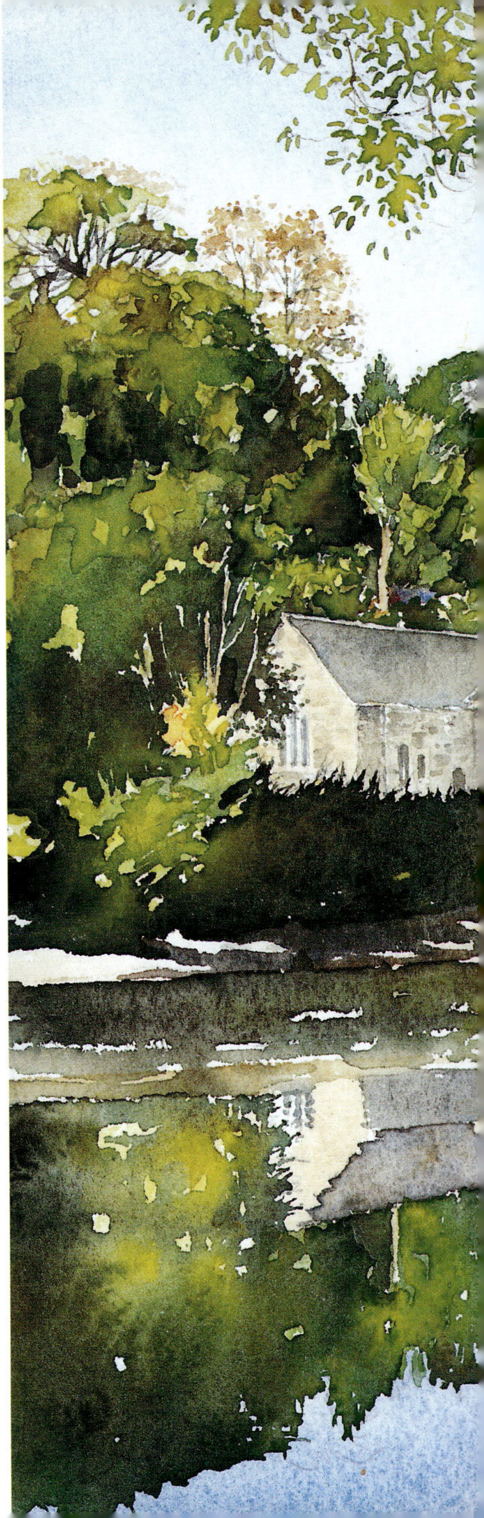

King Harry Ferry (above) and St. just in Roseland

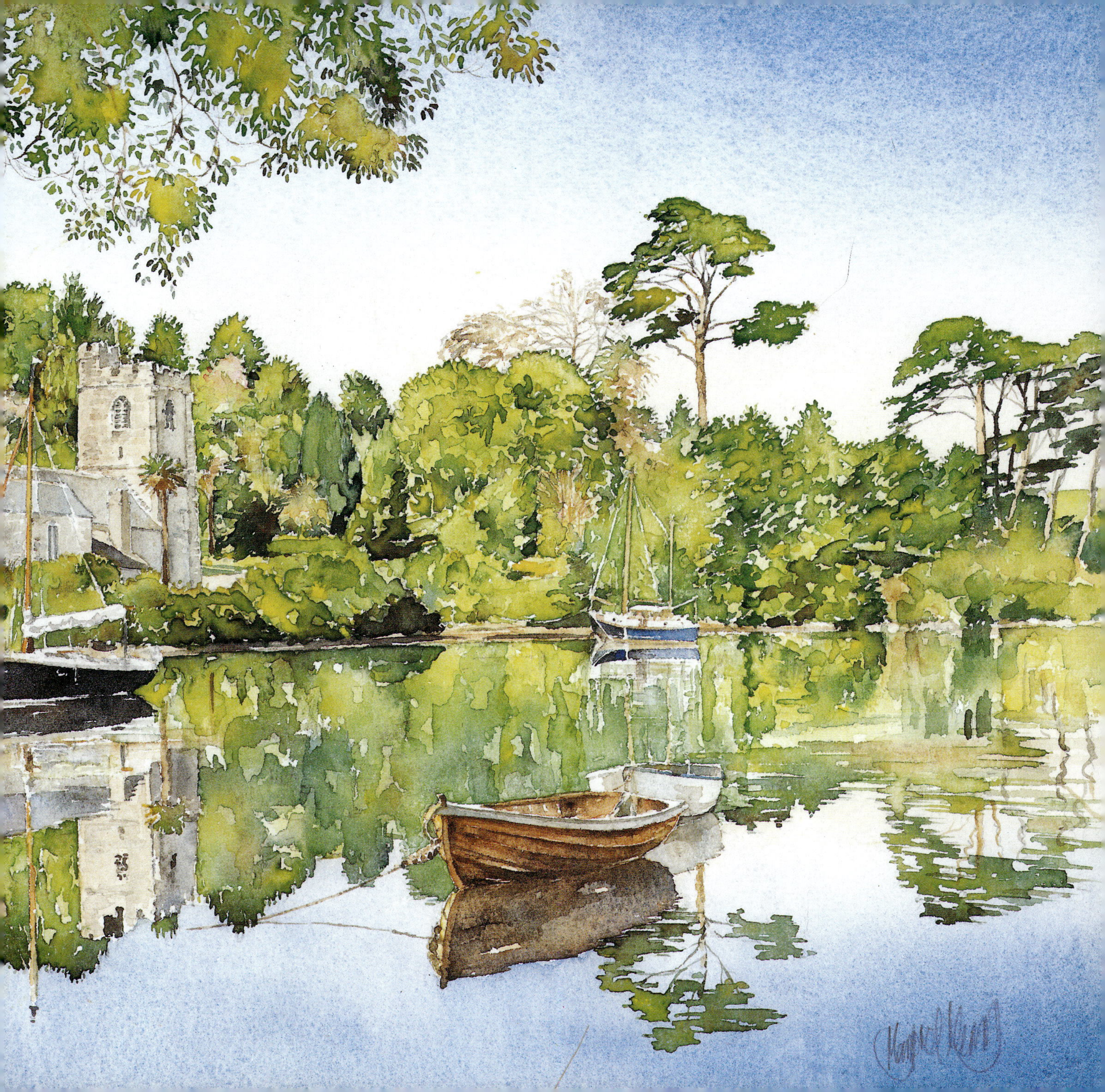

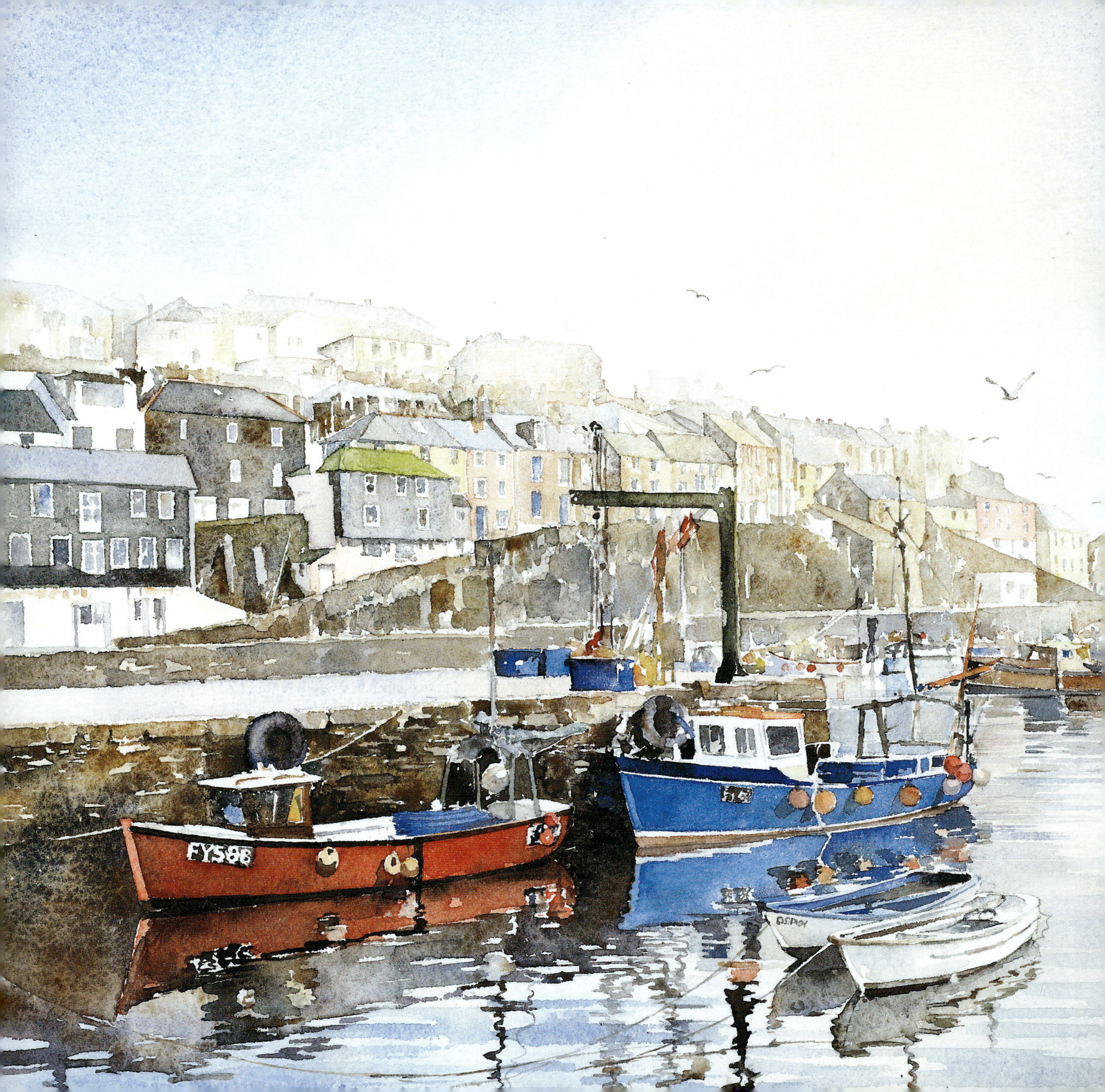

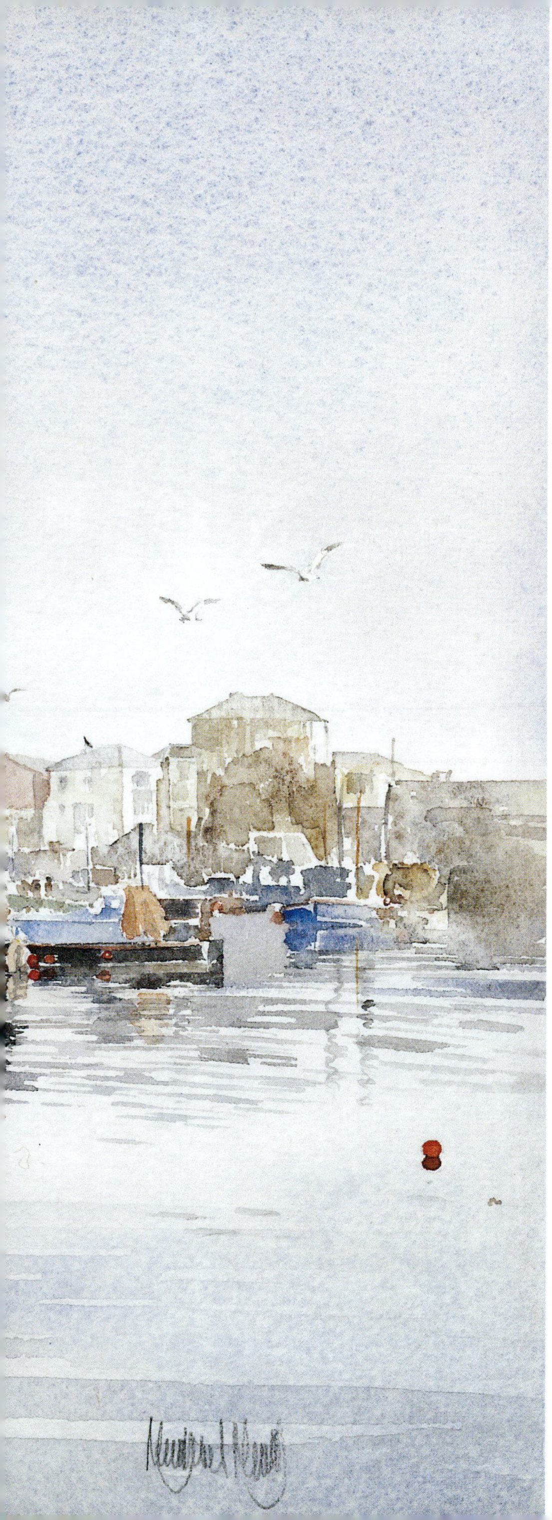

If I had to choose a harbour which most typified Cornwall, I would have to pick Mevagissey; certainly, I have painted it more than any other. When you are presented with a subject which is such a confusion of colour it is difficult to know what to paint and what to leave out so for this picture I have toned down the entire scene by making use of soft, early morning light.

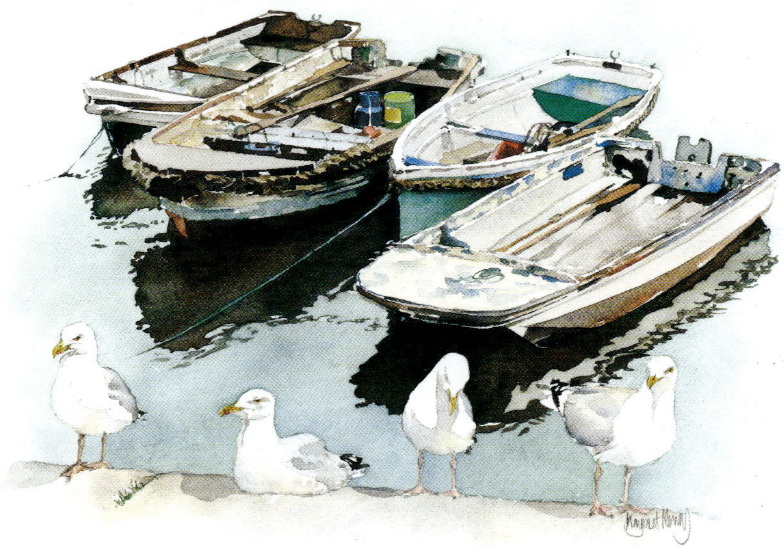

Mevagissey

ST. AUSTELL TO FOWEY

Before Charlestown was discovered by the film industry, it was a quiet little port which did not throng with the visitors it attracts today. Fortunately, it has not lost any of its charm and the tall ships moored along the jetties create an atmosphere that deceive you into thinking you have travelled back in time. I wanted to capture the romance of bygone times and the rosy light of a January morning, so I chose pastel as my medium for the main picture here.

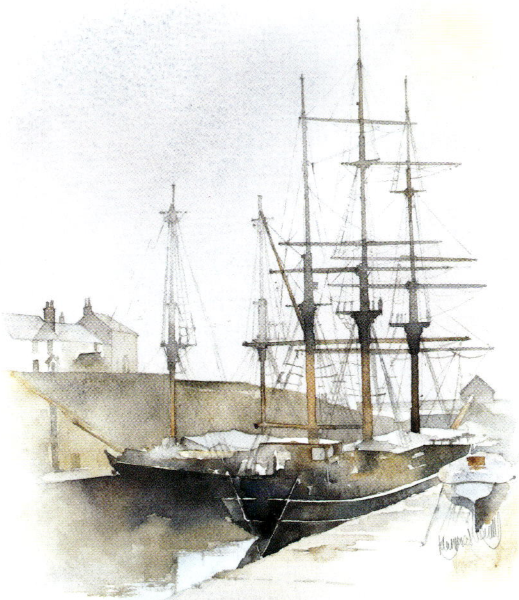

Charlestown

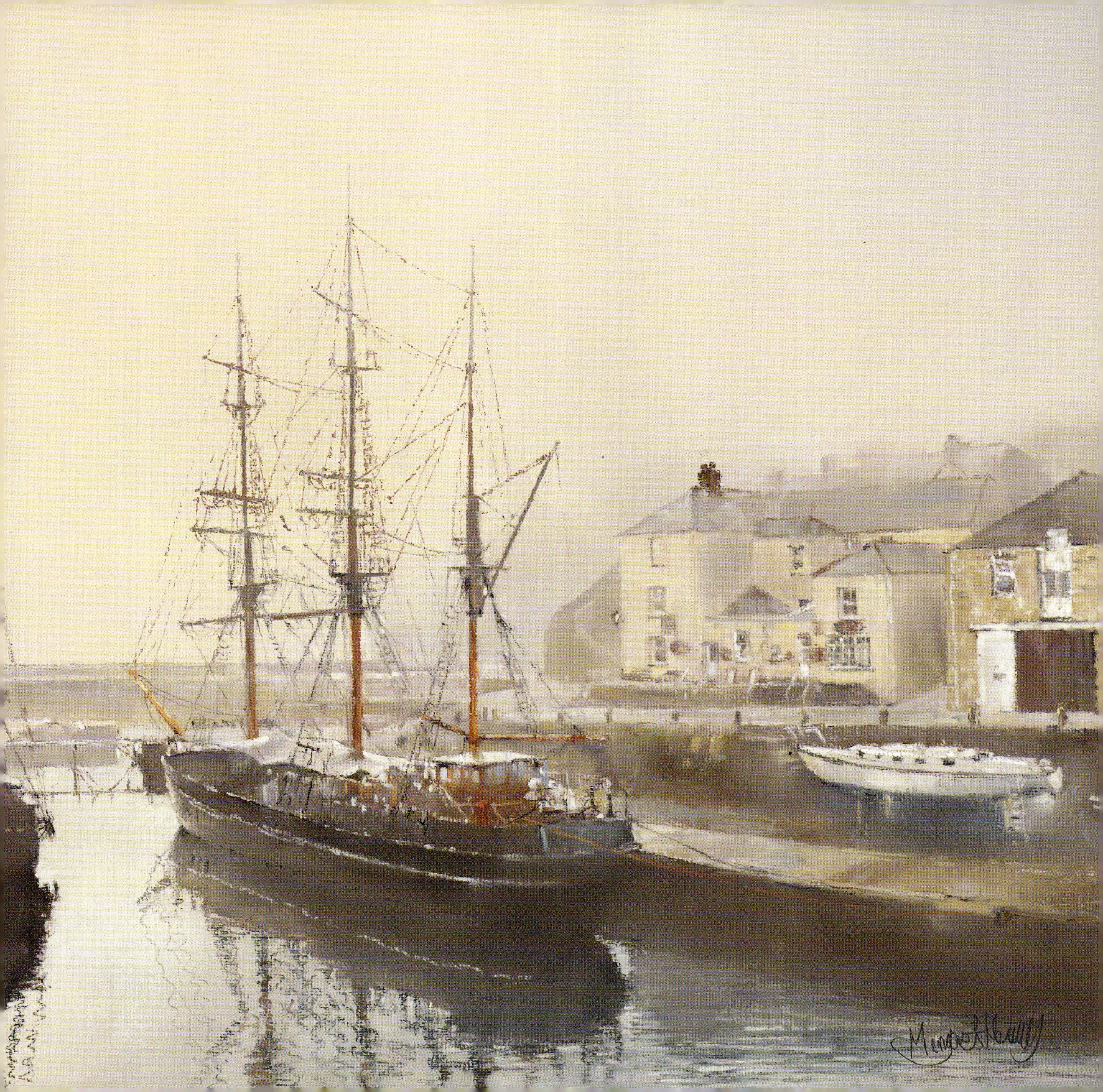

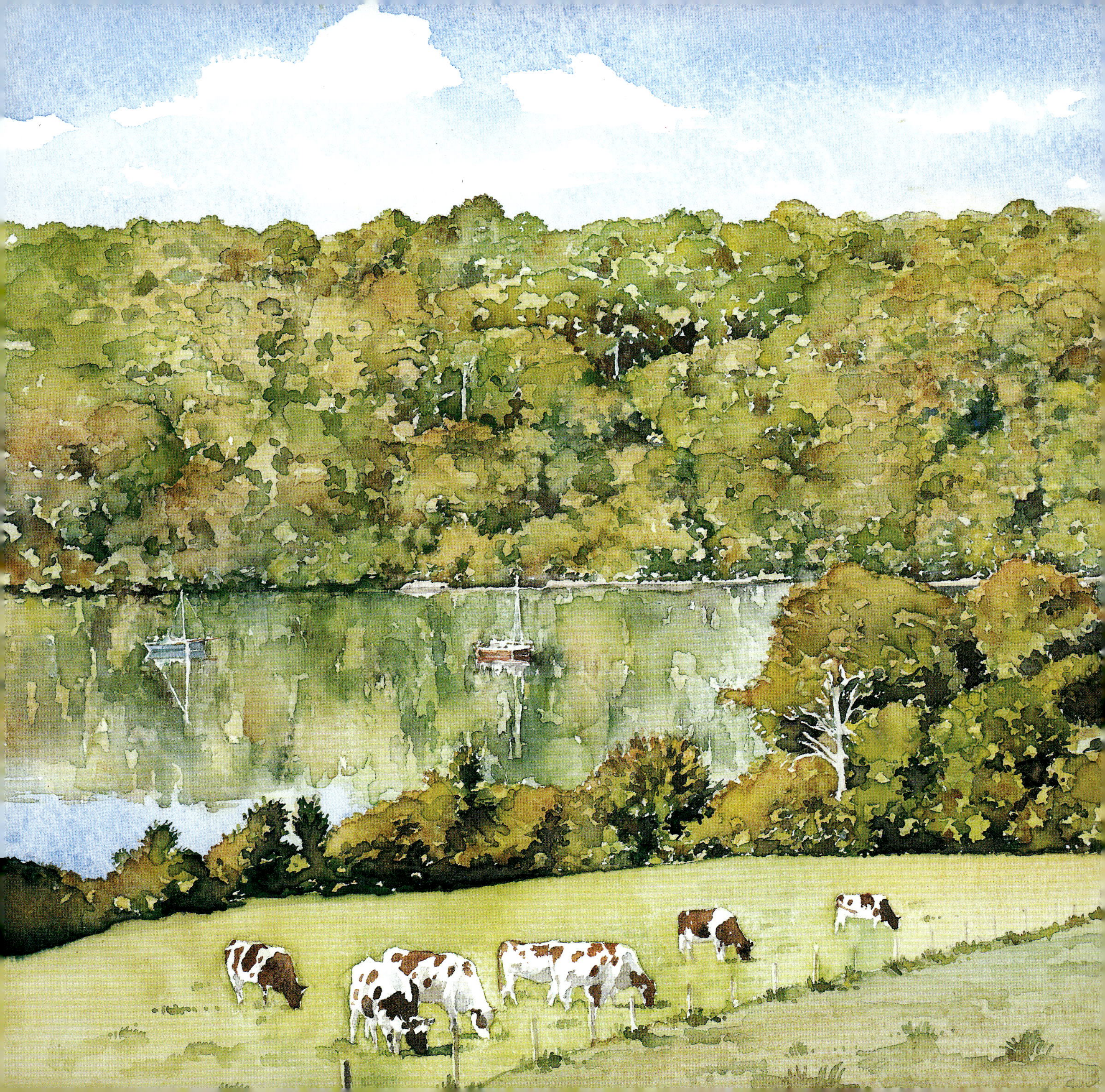

Below sloping fields, in an utterly beautiful setting on the curve of the river, is this view of the waterside church of St. Winnow. This picure was painted on a September morning with the trees just beginning to take on autumnal colour. Walking from Lerryn by way of woods and fields and foreshore, you are able to appreciate the wealth of wildlife supported by the river and its surrounds.

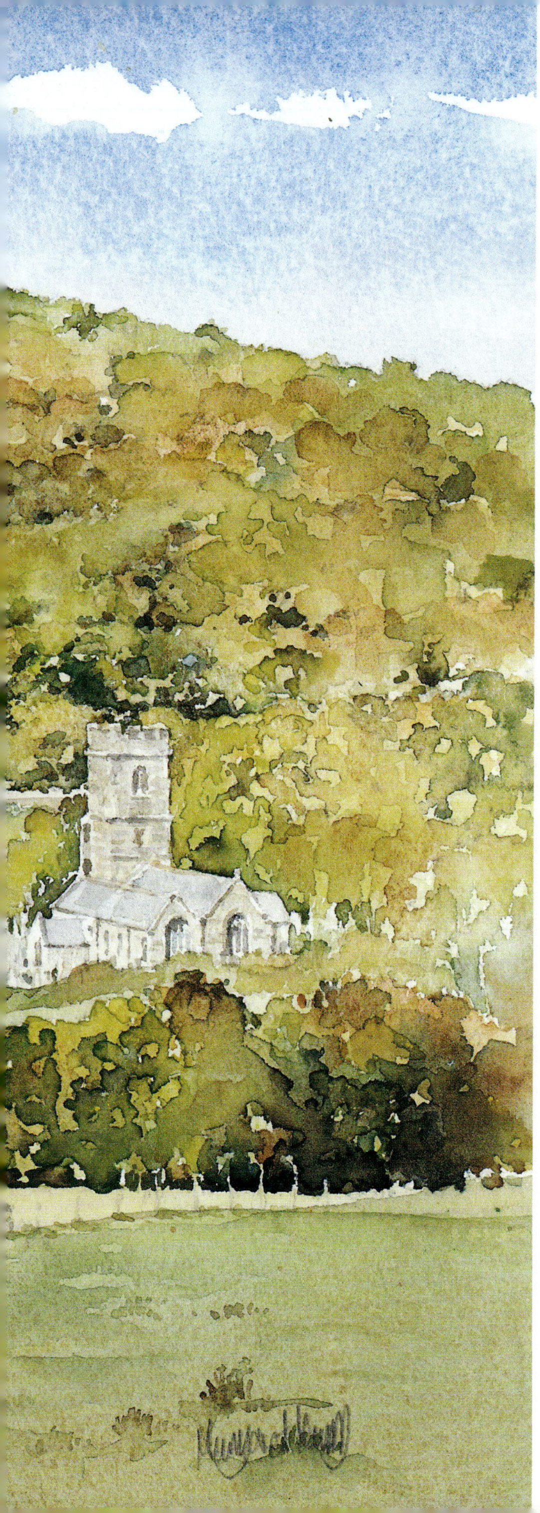

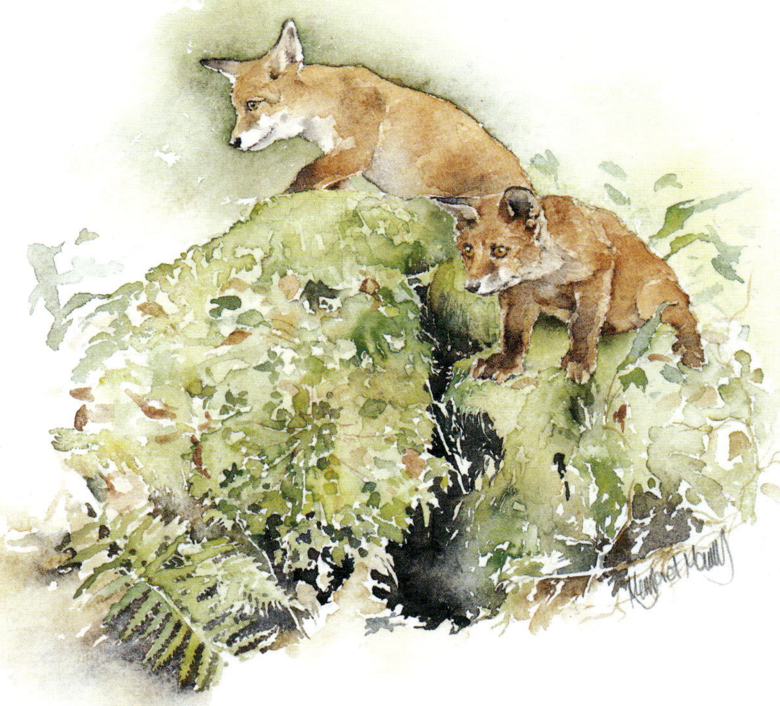

St. Winnow

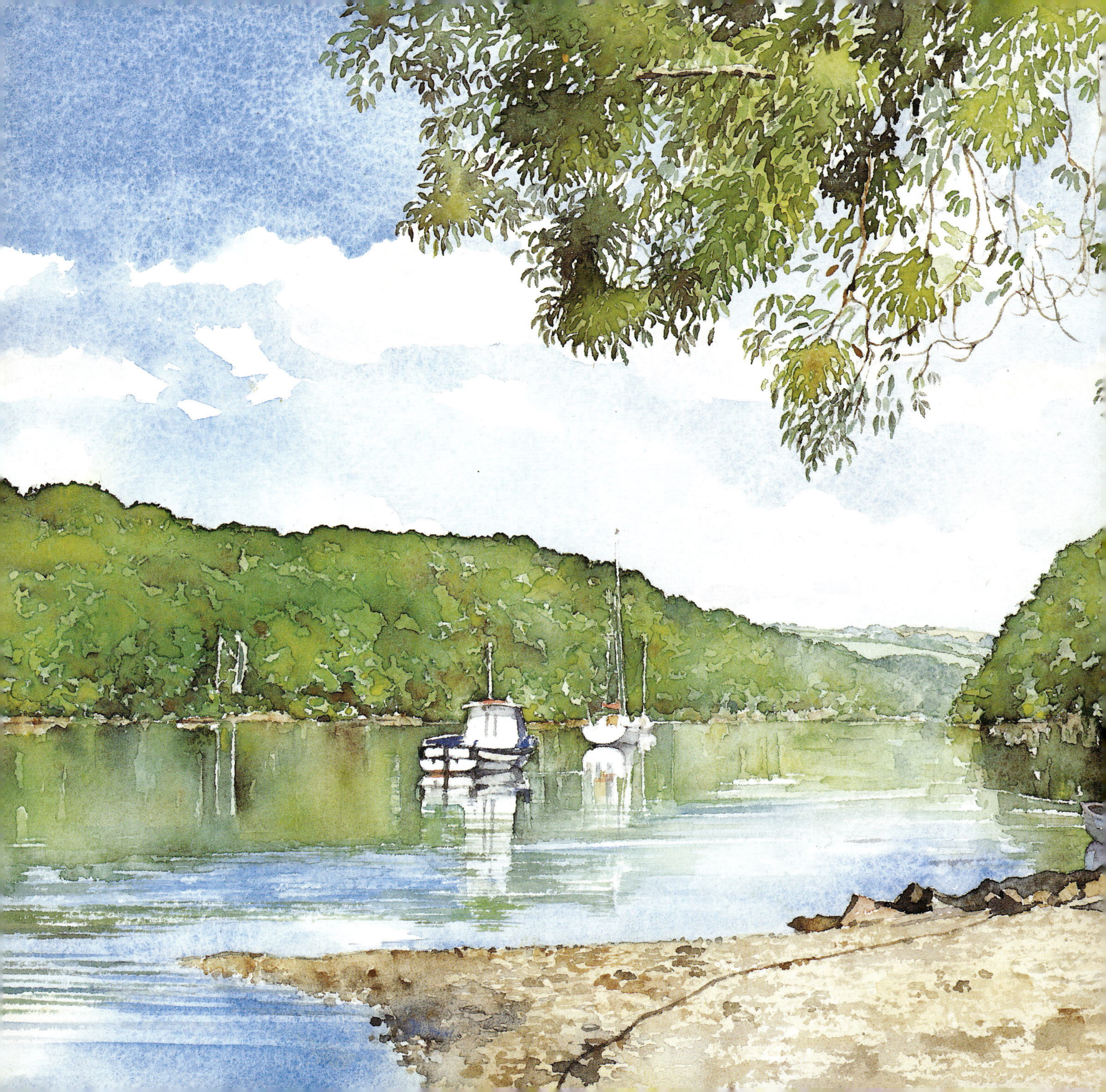

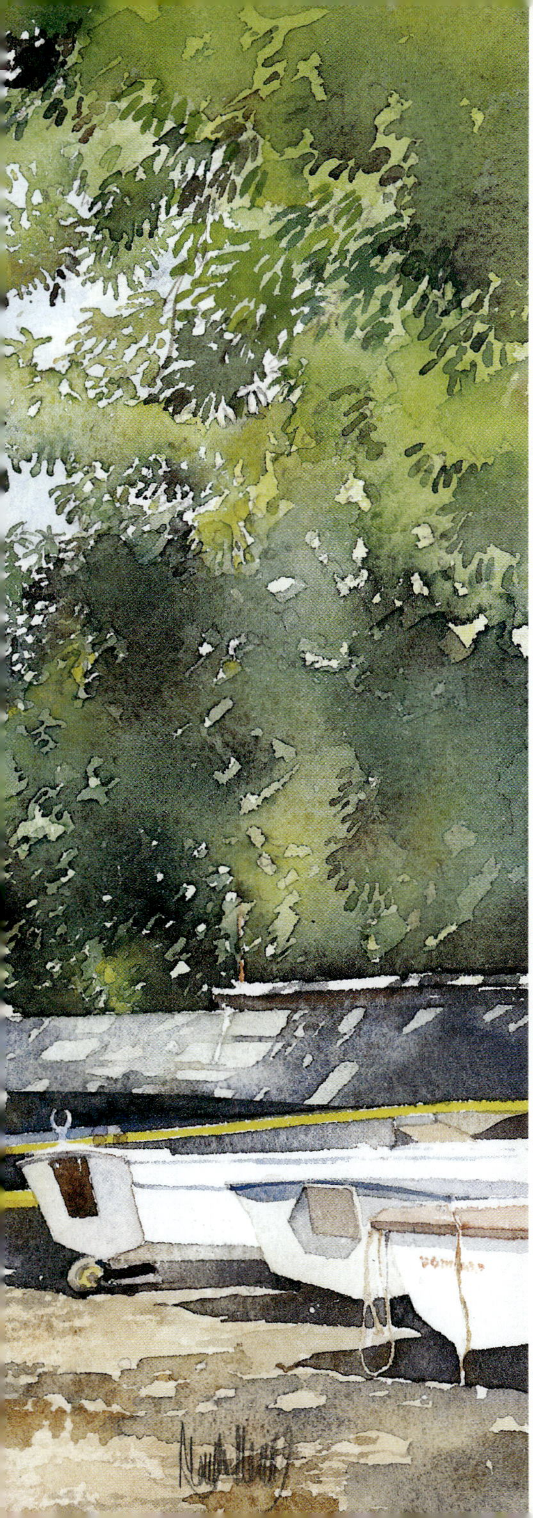

This is another view of the river at St. Winnow. Here, the perfect tranquility may be broken by a strange, distant rumbling which, growing louder, turns out to be a goods train trundling out of the woods on a hidden track along the water's edge on the opposite side of the river.

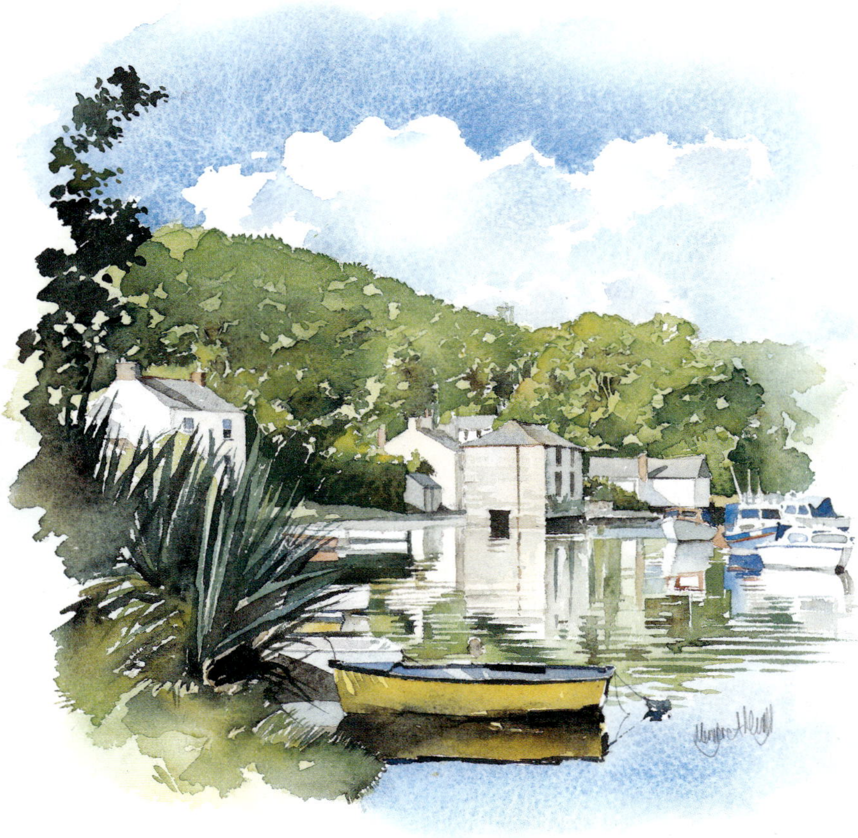

The river at St. Winnow and Lerryn (above)

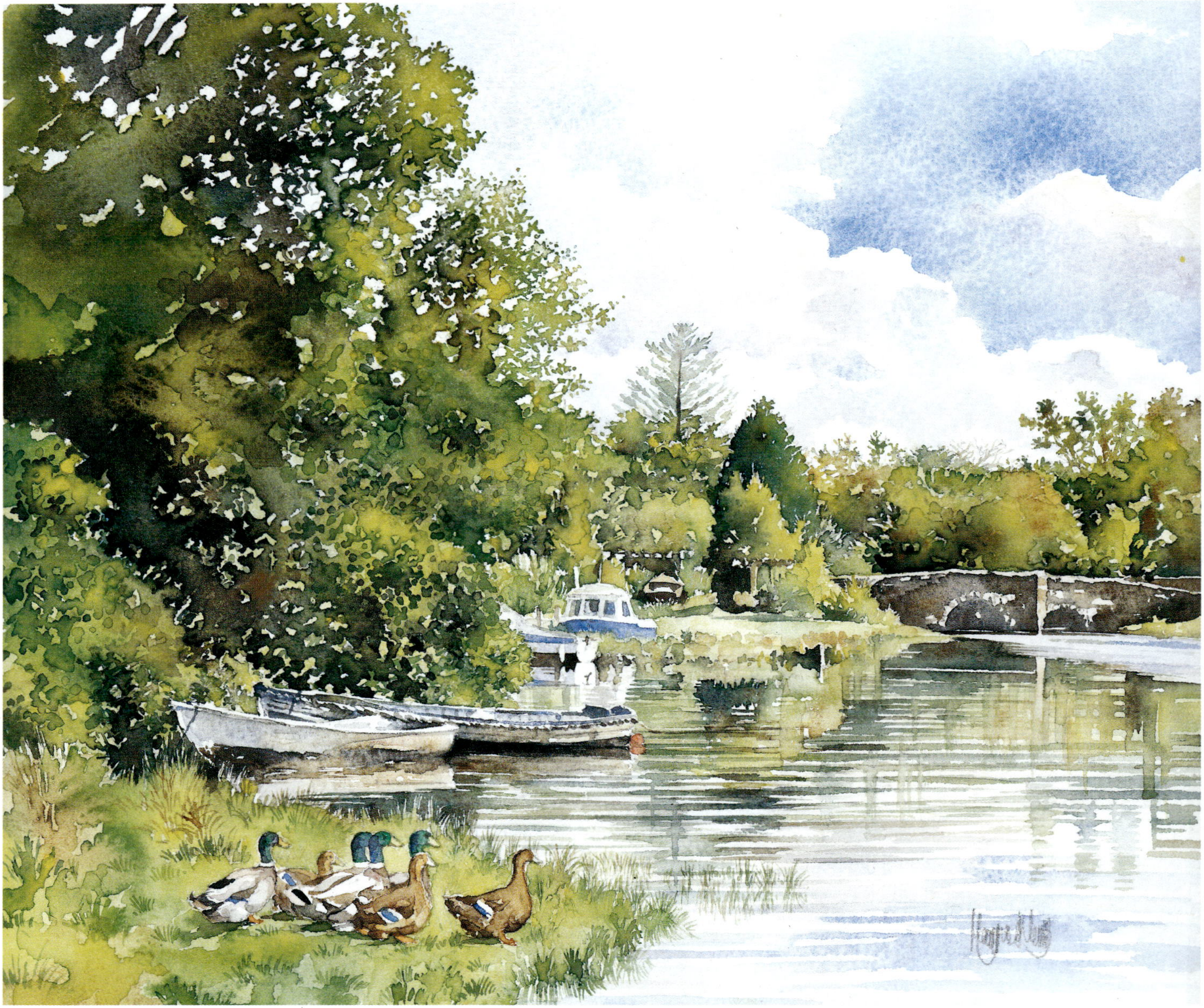

Lerryn

Lerryn is a delightful tidal reach of boats and cottages. Stepping stones take you across the river at low tide but at high water you must use the bridge which, together with the numerous resident ducks, is very much a feature of the village.

I am pleased that Fowey has not lost any of its character nor its buildings their quaint appearance over the years; I have always enjoyed painting here. This is my favourite view, looking across the river to Bodinnick.

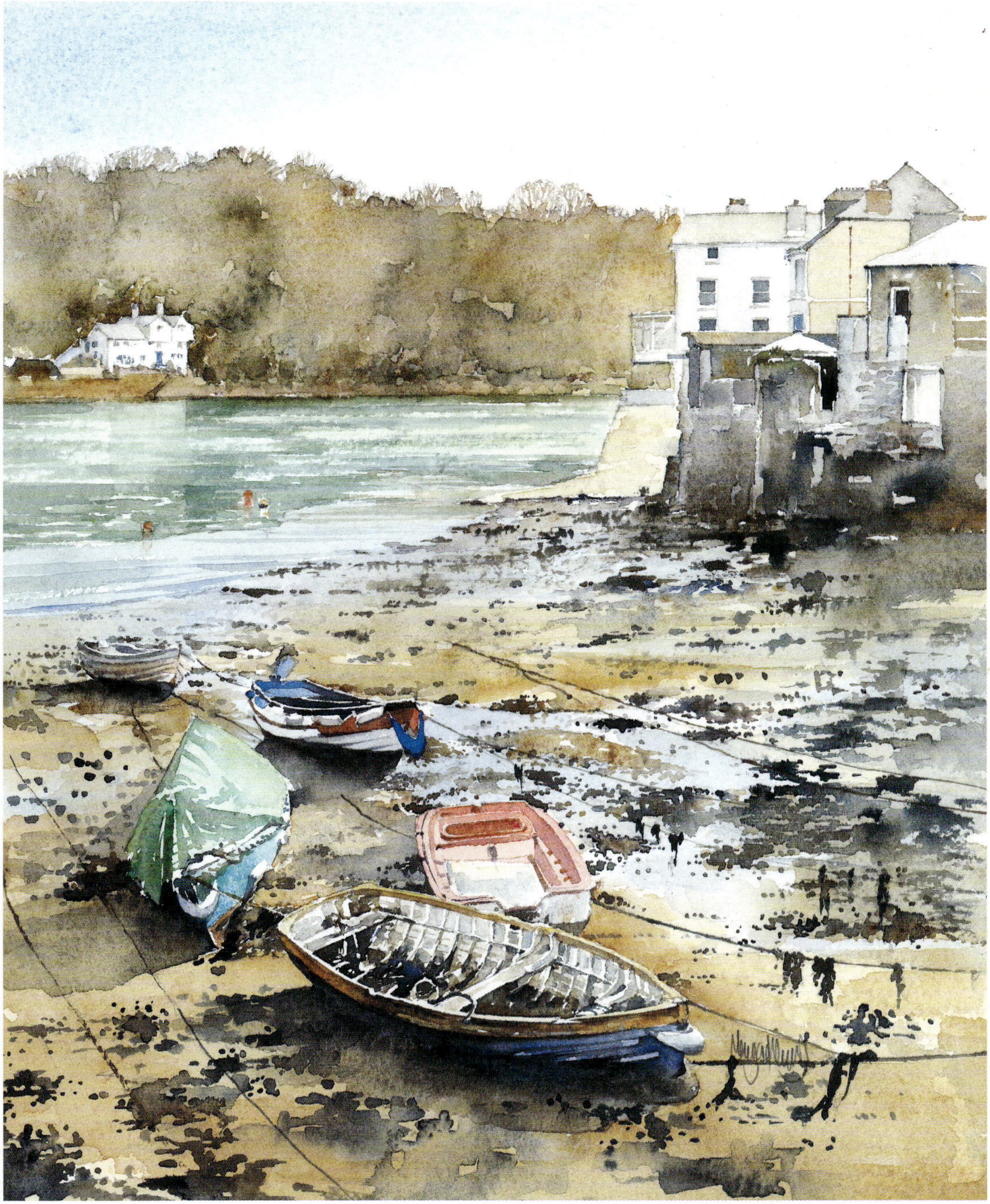

Fowey

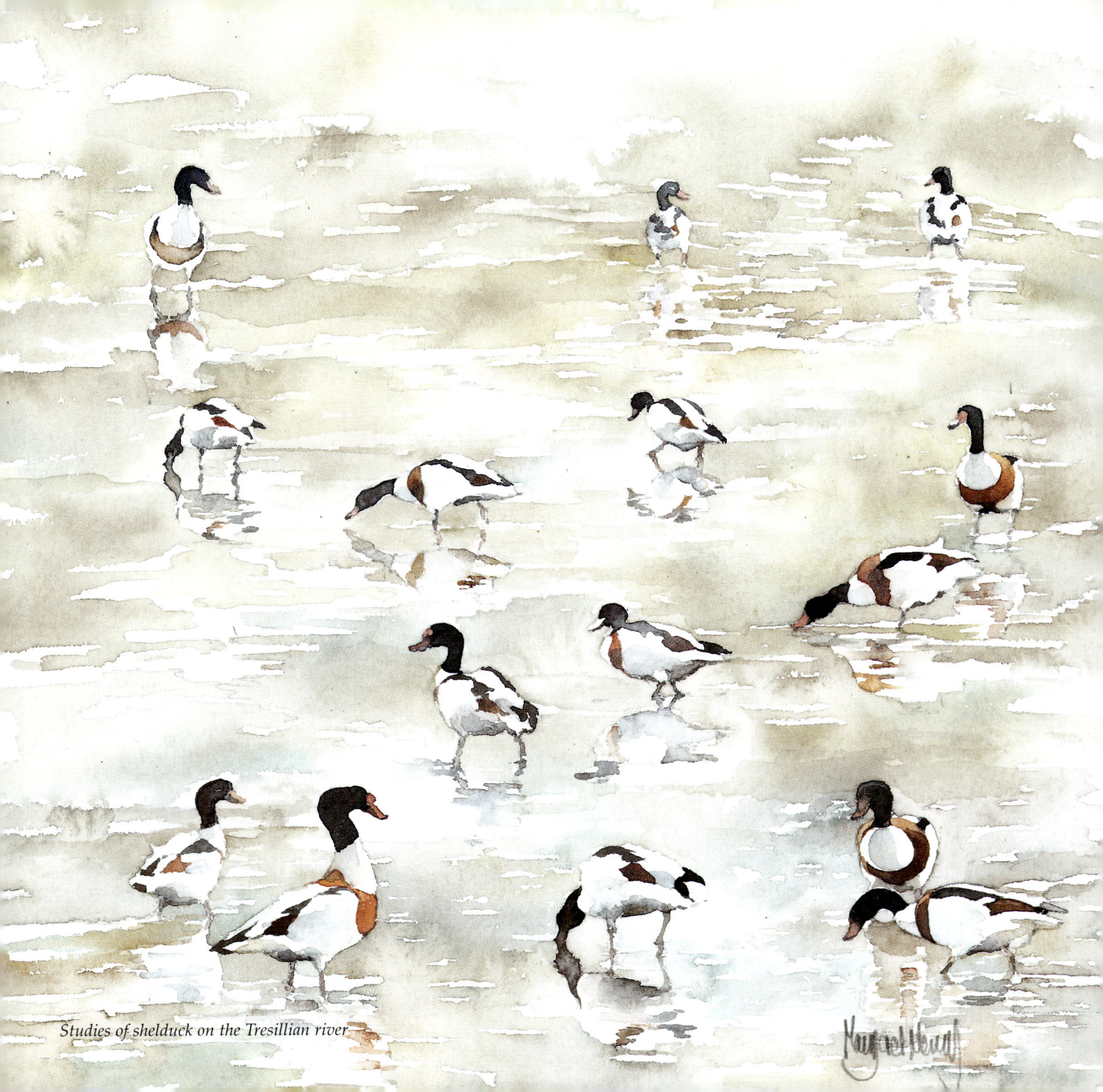

Studies of shelduck on the Tresillian river